HARCOURT HORIZONS

United States History:

Beginnings

Activity Book

Teacher's Edition

Orlando   Austin   Chicago   New York   Toronto   London   San Diego

Visit *The Learning Site!*
www.harcourtschool.com

Printed in the United States of America

The activities in this book reinforce social studies concepts and skills in **Harcourt Horizons: United States History: Beginnings**. There is one activity for every lesson and skill in the Pupil Edition. Copies of the activity pages appear with answers in the Teacher's Edition. In addition to activities, this book also contains reproductions of the graphic organizers that appear in the chapter reviews in the Pupil Edition. Multiple-choice test preparation pages for student practice are also provided. A blank multiple-choice answer sheet can be found after these contents pages.

Contents

Introduction

·UNIT·

1

Chapter 1

Chapter 2

Name _____   Date _____

Multiple-Choice
Answer Sheet

Number your answers to match the questions on the test preparation page.

——	Ⓐ	Ⓑ	Ⓒ	Ⓓ
——	Ⓕ	Ⓖ	Ⓗ	Ⓙ
——	Ⓐ	Ⓑ	Ⓒ	Ⓓ
——	Ⓕ	Ⓖ	Ⓗ	Ⓙ
——	Ⓐ	Ⓑ	Ⓒ	Ⓓ

——	Ⓐ	Ⓑ	Ⓒ	Ⓓ
——	Ⓕ	Ⓖ	Ⓗ	Ⓙ
——	Ⓐ	Ⓑ	Ⓒ	Ⓓ
——	Ⓕ	Ⓖ	Ⓗ	Ⓙ
——	Ⓐ	Ⓑ	Ⓒ	Ⓓ

——	Ⓐ	Ⓑ	Ⓒ	Ⓓ
——	Ⓕ	Ⓖ	Ⓗ	Ⓙ
——	Ⓐ	Ⓑ	Ⓒ	Ⓓ
——	Ⓕ	Ⓖ	Ⓗ	Ⓙ
——	Ⓐ	Ⓑ	Ⓒ	Ⓓ

——	Ⓐ	Ⓑ	Ⓒ	Ⓓ
——	Ⓕ	Ⓖ	Ⓗ	Ⓙ
——	Ⓐ	Ⓑ	Ⓒ	Ⓓ
——	Ⓕ	Ⓖ	Ⓗ	Ⓙ
——	Ⓐ	Ⓑ	Ⓒ	Ⓓ

——	Ⓐ	Ⓑ	Ⓒ	Ⓓ
——	Ⓕ	Ⓖ	Ⓗ	Ⓙ
——	Ⓐ	Ⓑ	Ⓒ	Ⓓ
——	Ⓕ	Ⓖ	Ⓗ	Ⓙ
——	Ⓐ	Ⓑ	Ⓒ	Ⓓ

Name _____ Date _____

MAP AND GLOBE SKILLS
Read a Map

Directions Use the map to answer the questions that follow.

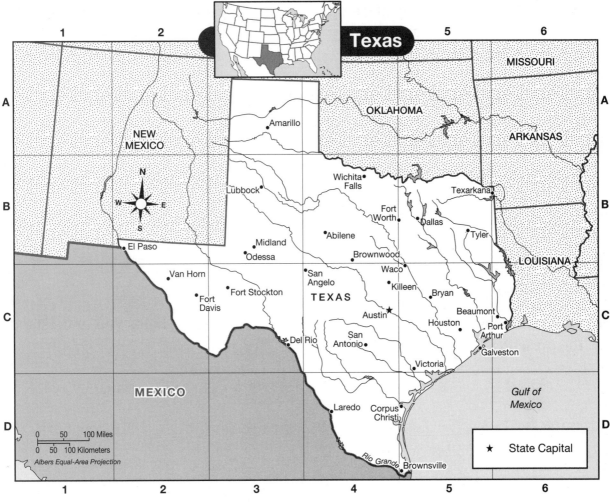

1. What is the capital of Texas? Austin

2. What states border Texas? New Mexico, Oklahoma, Arkansas, Louisiana

3. What cities are located in C5? Waco, Bryan, Houston, Victoria, Galveston

4. What bodies of water border Texas? the Gulf of Mexico and the Rio Grande

5. About how many miles is it from Fort Davis to El Paso if you drive through

   Van Horn? about 170 mi.

   What direction do you travel to get there? NW

6. What river forms the border between Texas and Mexico? the Rio Grande

Why History Matters

Directions Use the terms in the Word Bank to complete the sentences below.

history	oral history	historical empathy	analyze
chronology	point of view	frames of reference	

1 People's _____ frames of reference _____ are based on where people were when an event happened and how they were involved with that event.

2 _____ chronology _____ is the order in which events happened.

3 A person's _____ point of view _____ is based on his or her age, gender, class, background, and experiences.

4 Historians listen to and read records of _____ oral history _____ to help them understand past events.

5 Understanding _____ history _____ helps you understand the present.

READING SKILLS

Compare Primary and Secondary Sources

Directions Use Captain Charles Sigsbee's letter and the *New York Times* article to answer the questions below.

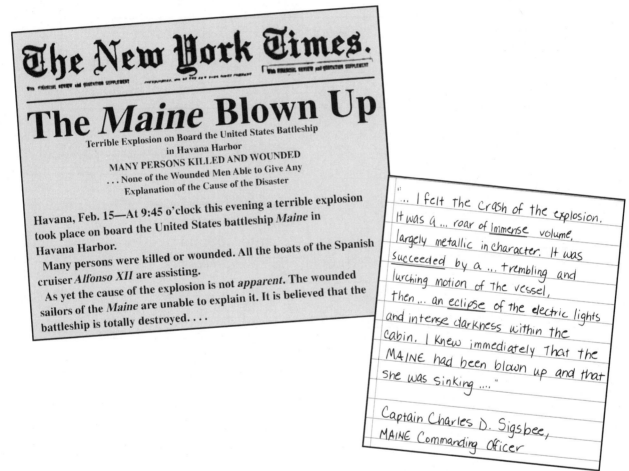

The New York Times.

The *Maine* Blown Up
Terrible Explosion on Board the United States Battleship in Havana Harbor
MANY PERSONS KILLED AND WOUNDED
. . . None of the Wounded Men Able to Give Any Explanation of the Cause of the Disaster

Havana, Feb. 15—At 9:45 o'clock this evening a terrible explosion took place on board the United States battleship *Maine* in Havana Harbor.

Many persons were killed or wounded. All the boats of the Spanish cruiser *Alfonso XII* are assisting.

As yet the cause of the explosion is not *apparent*. The wounded sailors of the *Maine* are unable to explain it. It is believed that the battleship is totally destroyed. . . .

... I felt the crash of the explosion. It was a ... roar of Immense volume, largely metallic in character. It was succeeded by a ... trembling and lurching motion of the vessel, then ... an eclipse of the electric lights and intense darkness within the cabin. I knew immediately that the MAINE had been blown up and that she was sinking ...."

Captain Charles D. Sigsbee,
MAINE Commanding Officer

---

1 What source lists where the explosion occurred? the newspaper article

2 How did Captain Sigsbee know the *Maine* was sinking?

He felt the ship trembling and lurching and saw the lights go out.

3 What does Captain Sigsbee's letter tell you that the *New York Times* article

does not? Captain Sigsbee's letter describes what it felt like inside the ship.

4 How is the tone of the newspaper article different from the tone of the letter?

The newspaper article is more factual, with less emotion.

Name _____ Date _____

Why Geography Matters

Geography is the study of the Earth's surface and the way people use it. Geographers use many different themes and topics to study a place. Understanding these themes and topics and their relationships will help you to better understand geography.

Directions Use the Word Bank to fill in the web and the question below.

Places and Regions	Geography	Location
Movement	Human Feature	Uses of Geography
Environment and Society	Human Systems	Physical Feature

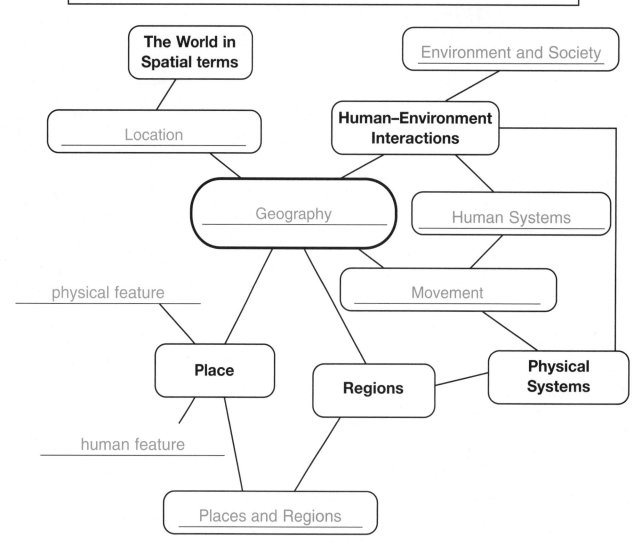

Knowing how to use maps, globes, and geographic tools helps you understand the

_____ uses of geography _____ and prepares you for life.

Name _____ Date _____

Why Economics, Civics, and Government Matter

Directions Read the flow chart and answer the questions below.

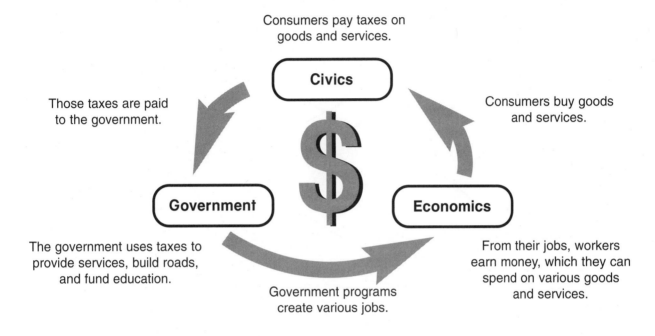

1 What happens when fewer jobs are available and unemployment goes up?

Consumers have less money and buy fewer goods and services, fewer

taxes are paid, and the government has less money to provide services.

2 What step happens between when the government creates jobs and when

consumers buy goods and services? Workers earn money which they can use

to buy goods and services.

3 What happens when the government raises taxes? The government has more

money to provide services, but consumers may not be able to afford to buy as

much.

4 What would happen if consumers did not pay taxes on goods and services?

The government would not have that money to provide services, build roads,

and fund education.

Land and Regions

Directions Look at each numbered place on the map. Find the word in the box that describes the place. Then write the word on the line with the same number.

sea level	basin	mountain range	plain
valley	volcano	piedmont	plateau

1 _____ volcano _____

2 _____ mountain range _____

3 _____ valley _____

4 _____ plateau _____

5 _____ plain _____

6 _____ sea level _____

Directions Show the meaning of the words *piedmont* and *plateau* by using each word in a sentence.

A piedmont is the area at or near the foot of a mountain. A plateau is a flat area

that stands high above the surrounding land.

_____

Use after reading Chapter 1, Lesson 1, pages 18–23.

MAP AND GLOBE SKILLS
Use Elevation Maps

Directions Study the elevation map and answer the questions below.

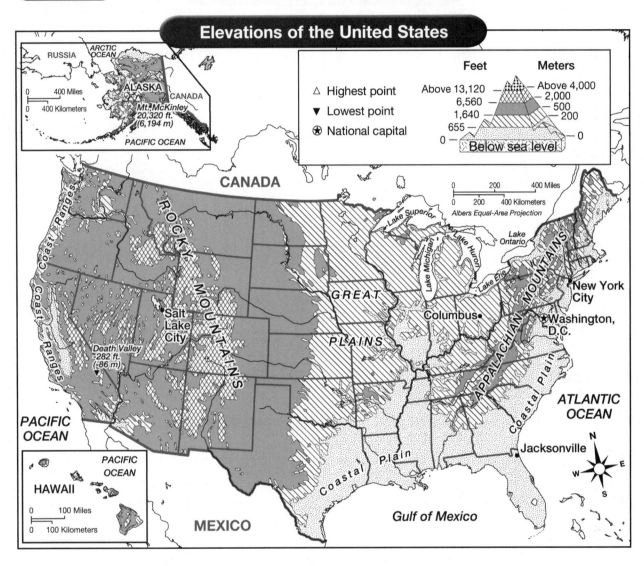

1 Which city has the higher elevation: Jacksonville, Florida, or Columbus, Ohio?

Columbus, Ohio

2 What is the elevation range of the Rocky Mountains? from 6,560 ft. to above

13,120 ft. (from 2,000 m to 4,000 m)

3 In what state can you find an inland location that is lower than sea level? What is

the name of the location? Death Valley in California

Bodies of Water

Directions Use the map to answer the questions below.

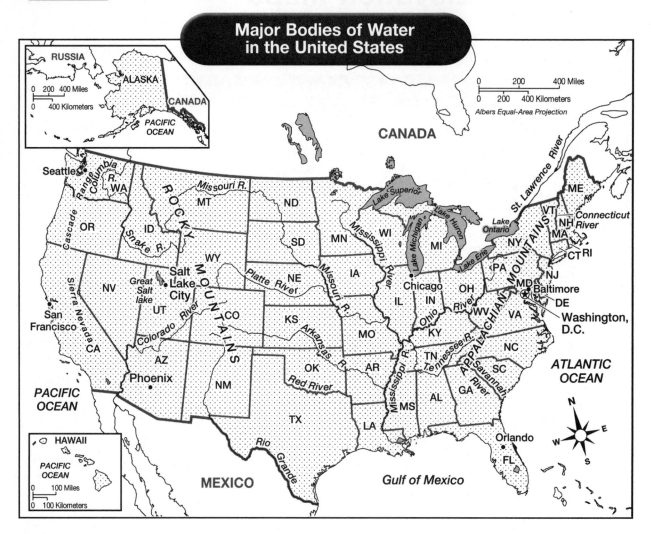

Major Bodies of Water in the United States

1 Name the Great Lakes. Lake Superior, Lake Michigan, Lake Huron, Lake Erie, Lake Ontario

2 Name the states that border the Gulf of Mexico. Texas, Louisiana, Mississippi, Alabama, Florida

3 Name three tributaries of the Mississippi River. possible answers: Missouri, Ohio, Arkansas Rivers

4 What states does the Arkansas River flow through? Arkansas, Oklahoma, Kansas, and Colorado

Climate and Vegetation Regions

Directions Use the map to fill in the chart below.

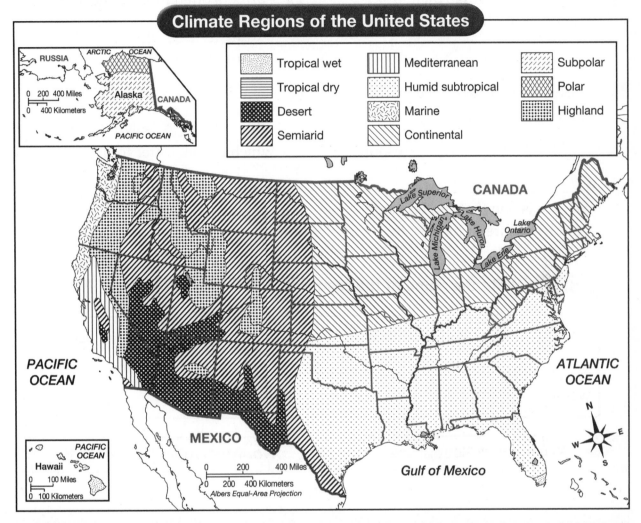

Climate Regions of the United States

Legend:
- Tropical wet
- Tropical dry
- Desert
- Semiarid
- Mediterranean
- Humid subtropical
- Marine
- Continental
- Subpolar
- Polar
- Highland

Place or Region	Climate Region
Southeastern United States	humid subtropical, tropical wet
Southwestern United States	desert, semiarid, highland, humid subtropical
Pacific Coast	Mediterranean, marine, semiarid, desert
Atlantic Coast	tropical wet, humid subtropical, continental
Alaska	polar, subpolar
Hawaii	tropical wet

Name _____ Date _____

Using the Land

Directions Write the correct answer in the space provided.

1 When people change their environment, they _____modify_____ it.

2 A resource that cannot be made again by nature or people is called a _____nonrenewable_____ resource.

3 A _____renewable_____ resource is one that can be made again by nature or by people.

4 Farmers often modify the soil by adding _____fertilizer_____ to grow better crops.

5 Some farmers modify their land with _____irrigation_____, which brings water to dry areas.

Directions Write the name of the resource in the correct column.

air	iron	trees	zinc	fish
sunlight	oil	natural gas	plants	limestone
water	gold	copper	coal	wind

Renewable Resources	Nonrenewable Resources
air	gold
sunlight	coal
trees	natural gas
plants	iron
water	copper
fish	zinc
wind	oil
	limestone

Use after reading Chapter 1, Lesson 4, pages 40–43.

Name _____ Date _____

Where People Live and Work

Directions Read each clue. Then use the clues to complete the word puzzle below.

relative location	crossroads	suburban	rural
metropolitan	railroad	farm	economic

ACROSS

3 The location of a place compared to one or more other places

5 A place where crops are raised

6 Kind of area made up of a city and its suburbs

7 A place where two roads or railroads intersect

DOWN

1 Kind of area surrounding a large city

2 A system that moves goods overland

3 Kind of area located in the country, away from cities

4 Region named for the work done or product made within it

													1S	
		2R											U	
3R	E	L	A	T	I	V	**4**E	L	O	C	A	T	I	O	N	B
U		I				C							U	
R		L				O							R	
A		R				N							B	
L		O				O							A	
	5F	A	R	M		**6**M	E	T	R	O	P	O	L	I	T	A	N
		D				I							
						7C	R	O	S	S	R	O	A	D	S

MAP AND GLOBE SKILLS
Use Latitude and Longitude

Directions Location is important to people choosing a place to live. People may choose to live and work near a coast or near a major transportation route. Use the map to fill in the chart below.

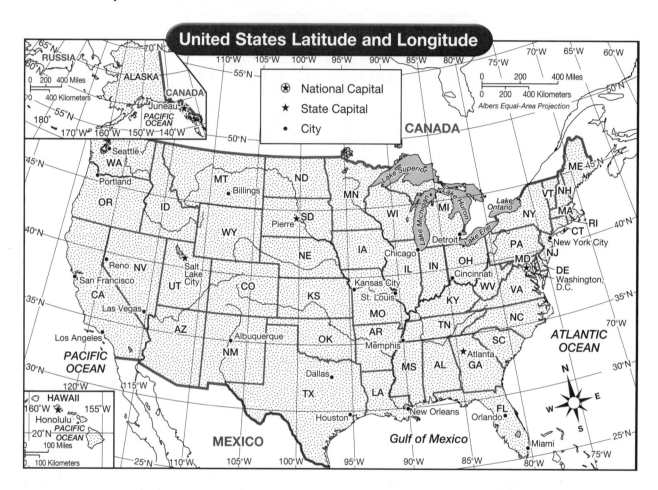

United States Latitude and Longitude

City	Latitude	Longitude
New York City, NY	41° N	74° W
Los Angeles, CA	34° N	119° W
Chicago, IL	42° N	88° W
New Orleans, LA	30° N	90° W

Regions of the United States

Directions Complete this graphic organizer to show that you have identified the main idea and supporting details in this chapter.

SUPPORTING DETAILS

Cultural regions reflect the customs and beliefs of the main group of people who live there.

SUPPORTING DETAILS

Economic regions are based on the work people do or the products they make.

MAIN IDEA

The United States can be divided into regions based on people's activities.

SUPPORTING DETAILS

In political regions, people share a government and have the same leaders.

SUPPORTING DETAILS

Population regions are based on where people live.

1 Test Preparation

Directions Read each question and choose the best answer. Then fill in the circle for the answer you have chosen. Be sure to fill in the circle completely.

1 What natural region is located at or near the foot of a mountain?

Ⓐ peak

Ⓑ hill

Ⓒ piedmont

Ⓓ humidity

2 Which of these is **not** the name of a landform?

Ⓕ plain

Ⓖ climate

Ⓗ mountain

Ⓙ valley

3 Which of these cause ocean currents?

Ⓐ location

Ⓑ elevation

Ⓒ precipitation

Ⓓ wind

4 Places in the rain shadow of a mountain receive very little—

Ⓕ sunlight.

Ⓖ precipitation.

Ⓗ wind.

Ⓙ temperature.

5 Another name for *grassland* is—

Ⓐ prairie.

Ⓑ mesquite.

Ⓒ lichens.

Ⓓ tundra.

Use after reading Chapter 1, pages 16–53.

The First to Arrive

Directions Read the list of statements below about the arrival of ancient peoples in the Americas. In the spaces provided, write *LB* if a statement refers to the land bridge theory, *EA* if it refers to the early-arrival theory, or *O* if it refers to origin theory.

1 __O__ The Blackfoot people tell a story of Old Man the Creator.

2 __LB__ Some scientists believe that between 12,000 and 40,000 years ago, Asian hunting groups reached present-day Alaska.

3 __EA__ Recent discoveries support the idea that ancient peoples came by boat to the Americas.

4 __EA__ Archaeologists in Brazil have discovered artifacts that may be 30,000 years old.

5 __O__ According to the Hurons, land was formed from soil found in a turtle's claws.

6 __O__ There are many people today who believe that the first Americans did not come from Asia or anywhere else.

7 __LB__ Following a path between glaciers, hunters slowly made their way farther into the Americas.

8 __EA__ At Meadowcroft Rock Shelter archaeologists discovered a few artifacts that are more than 19,000 years old.

9 __O__ Many present-day Native Americans believe that their people have always lived in the Americas.

10 __LB__ After thousands of years, Asian hunters reached what is today Alaska.

11 __EA__ In Monte Verde, Chile, archaeologists uncovered artifacts, animal bones, and a child's foot print that had been there for at least 13,000 years.

12 __LB__ At several different times the level of the oceans dropped causing dry land to appear between Asia and North America.

Name _____ Date _____

CHART AND GRAPH SKILLS
Read Time Lines

Directions The time line on this page lists events that happened in the Americas. Study the time line and then answer the questions below.

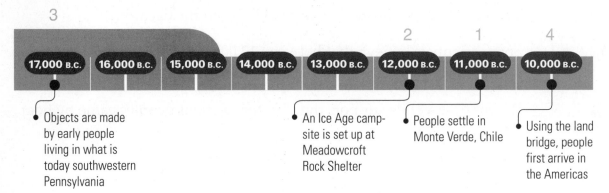

1. Artifacts found in Monte Verde, Chile, provide proof that people were there as

   long ago as _11,000 B.C._____.

2. Artifacts found at the Meadowcroft Rock Shelter suggest that people were

   living there in _12,000 B.C._____.

3. The oldest objects found at Meadowcroft Rock Shelter date back to

   _17,000 B.C._____.

4. The land-bridge theory says people first arrived in the Americas around

   _10,000 B.C._____.

Name _____ Date _____

Ancient Indians

Directions Use the Word Bank below to complete a paragraph about the different cultures of the Olmecs, Maya, Mound Builders, and Anasazi.

technology	nomads	Mound Builders	agriculture	civilization	extinct
Anasazi	classes	slaves	pueblos	tribes	

    The Olmec _____ civilization _____ lived in what is now southeastern Mexico. Because the Olmecs remained in one place, they were not

considered _____ nomads _____ . The Olmecs shared their ideas with

other cultures, or _____ tribes _____ , such as the Maya. The Olmecs

and Maya were divided into separate social _____ classes _____ , based upon people's occupations. At the bottom of Mayan society were

_____ slaves _____ , or people forced to work against their will. At about the same time, a group of Native Americans began building a society in what is today the southeastern United States. These people were known as

_____ Mound Builders _____ because of the earthen mounds they built as places of burial or worship. Hundreds of years later, a group called the

_____ Anasazi _____ built a society in what is today the southwestern United States. In this society, people lived in groups of houses built closely

together. These houses were called _____ pueblos _____ , the Spanish word for "village."

Name _____ Date _____

MAP AND GLOBE SKILLS
Use a Cultural Map

Directions Use the map to answer the following questions.

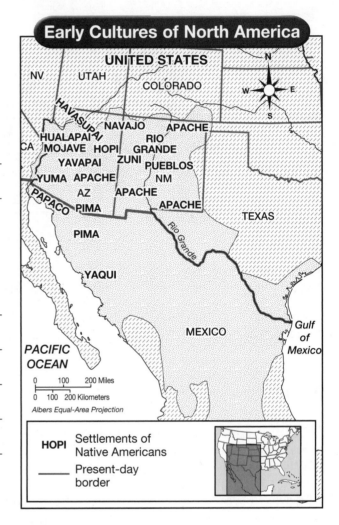

Early Cultures of North America

UNITED STATES
NV UTAH COLORADO
HAVASUPAI
HUALAPAI NAVAJO APACHE
CA MOJAVE HOPI RIO GRANDE
YAVAPAI ZUNI PUEBLOS
YUMA APACHE NM
AZ APACHE
PAPAGO PIMA APACHE
PIMA TEXAS
Rio Grande
YAQUI
MEXICO Gulf of Mexico
PACIFIC OCEAN
0 100 200 Miles
0 100 200 Kilometers
Albers Equal-Area Projection

HOPI Settlements of Native Americans
_____ Present-day border

1 According to the map, Native Americans of the Desert Southwest lived in parts of which present-day states? _Arizona and New Mexico_

_____

2 What generalization can you make about the location of settlements in the Desert Southwest?

Settlements were spread fairly

evenly across the present-day

states of Arizona and New Mexico

and usually were located near

water.

3 Why do you think the Navajos learned certain customs from the Hopis rather than from the Pima?

The Navajos lived closer to the Hopis than they did to the Pimas.

_____

4 What generalization can you make about the ways of life of Native Americans

who lived in the Southwest? _To cope with desert heat and little rainfall,_

the people built their homes near a source of water they could use

to irrigate their crops.

The Desert Southwest

Directions On the blanks provided, write the word or name that best completes each sentence. Some letters in your answers will have numbers underneath them. Write these letters on the numbered blanks below, and you will find the name of a region in the United States.

1 Many Native Americans who lived in the __d__ __e__ __s__ __e__ __r__ __t__
                                                                    1

were able to change the way they lived and adjust to the land and its resources.

2 Native American tribes such as the Hopis and

Zunis lived in __p__ __u__ __e__ __b__ __l__ __o__ __s__ .
                                                    2

3 They learned that by growing a __s__ __u__ __r__ __p__ __l__ __u__ __s__ of food
                                                        3
they could survive during times of harsh weather.

4 Many of the crops grown by Native Americans were

__s__ __t__ __a__ __p__ __l__ __e__ foods such as corn, beans, and squash.
        4

5 The Hopis worshiped many gods and spirits, including

__k__ __a__ __c__ __h__ __i__ __n__ __a__ __s__ , who were believed to visit
                        5
their world once a year.

6 Around the year 1025, the Hopis were joined on their lands by

__n__ __e__ __w__ __c__ __o__ __m__ __e__ __r__ __s__ , such as the Navajos.
                6

7 The Navajos settled in an area known as the __F__ __o__ __u__ __r__

__C__ __o__ __r__ __n__ __e__ __r__ __s__ region, where parts of present-day
                            7
Arizona, Colorado, New Mexico, and Utah meet.

8 The Navajos learned many customs from the Hopis, including how to build

dome-shaped shelters called __h__ __o__ __g__ __a__ __n__ __s__ .
                                                            8

9 The Navajos' use of Hopi ways was an example of their ability to

__a__ __d__ __a__ __p__ __t__ to desert life.
                        9

__s__	__o__	__u__	__t__	__h__	__w__	__e__	__s__	__t__
1	2	3	4	5	6	7	8	9

The Northwest Coast and the Arctic

Directions Complete the following chart by comparing and contrasting the ways of life of the Northwest Coast and Arctic Indians, and then answer the questions that follow.

Northwest Coast Indians	Arctic Indians
lived in a land of rivers and forests	lived in a land of snow and ice
lived in wooden houses	lived in igloos, tents, and huts
had many resources	had few resources
hunted salmon, other fish, and whales	hunted whales, seals, walrus, caribou
used trees to build shelter and make tools	used animal parts to build shelters and make tools

1 Contrast the living environments of the Northwest Coast and Arctic Indians.

The Northwest Coast Indians lived in a land of rivers and forests, while the

Arctic Indians lived in a land of snow and ice.

2 Describe the resources that the Northwest Coast and Arctic Indians used for

building shelters and making tools. The Northwest Coast Indians used trees to

build shelters and make tools, while the Arctic Indians used animal parts to build

shelters and make tools.

3 Using the information from the chart as a guide, write a paragraph comparing and contrasting the ways of life of the Northwest Coast and Arctic Indians.

The Northwest Coast Indians lived in a land of rivers and forests. The forests

provided wood to build houses and make tools. They hunted whales and fish,

such as salmon. In contrast, the Arctic Indians lived in a land of snow and ice

with few resources. They lived in igloos, tents, and huts and used animal parts to

make shelter and tools. Like the Northwest Coast Indians, the Arctic Indians

hunted whales in addition to seal, walrus, and caribou.

Name _____   Date _____

The Plains

Directions Match the items below to the buffalo parts from which they were made. You will use some parts more than once. Then answer the questions.

A. hides

B. stomach

C. hair

D. bones and horns

E. meat

___A___ clothing

___B___ bags for water

___C___ cord

___D___ needles and tools

___A___ blankets

___E___ fresh or dried food

___A___ moccasins

___A___ tepee coverings

1 Of the parts listed above, which was used for the most purposes?

hides

2 What parts would the Plains Indians have used to make their shelters?

hides, bones and horns, and hair

3 What buffalo part do you think was most useful? Student responses will vary

but may indicate that meat was most important because of the need for food.

The Eastern Woodlands

Directions Read the paragraph. Then answer the questions that follow.

In the late 1500s, Iroquois villages often battled among themselves. Often, these battles grew out of small disputes that led to ill will between villages. According to tradition, a Huron named Deganawida believed that the battles must stop if the Iroquois tribes were to protect their ways of life from European newcomers. Deganawida persuaded a Mohawk leader named Hiawatha to join him in spreading the message throughout Iroquois country that "All shall receive the Great Law and labor together for the welfare of man."

The result of their effort was a confederation called the Iroquois League, made up of the Five Nations of the Seneca, the Cayuga, the Onondaga, the Oneida, and the Mohawk. A few years later a sixth nation, the Tuscarora, joined the confederacy.

Each nation in the league governed itself, and matters often were settled by unanimous vote. Very important matters, such as war, were left for discussion by a Great Council of 50 chiefs.

1 Who was Deganawida? According to tradition, he was a Huron who, with a Mohawk named Hiawatha, convinced the Iroquois tribes that they must stop their battles and work together to protect their ways of life.

2 What tribes belonged to the Iroquois League? the Seneca, the Cayuga, the Onondaga, the Oneida, the Mohawk, and later, the Tuscarora

3 How were decisions made by the Iroquois League? Each nation governed itself, but important issues, such as war, were decided by a Great Council of 50 chiefs.

4 What do you think Deganawida meant when he said "All shall receive the Great Law and labor together for the welfare of man"? He meant that if the nations joined together and worked for the common good all Iroquois would benefit.

Name _____ Date _____

CITIZENSHIP SKILLS
Resolve Conflict

Directions Complete the graphic organizer below. For each step, write the decisions that led to the formation of the Iroquois League.

ALL SIDES CLEARLY STATE WANTS AND NEEDS

Answers should reflect that the Iroquois had competing wants and needs for resources such as land, which prevented them from achieving lasting peace among tribes.

ALL SIDES DECIDE WHAT IS MOST IMPORTANT

Answers should reflect that the Five Nations sided with Deganawida and

Hiawatha in believing that lasting peace was most important.

ALL SIDES PLAN AND DISCUSS POSSIBLE COMPROMISES

Accept all answers indicating that a new governing body would help resolve various disputes while working toward the common good. Without such a governing

body, disputes likely would continue and lasting peace would not be achieved.

ALL SIDES PLAN A LASTING COMPROMISE

Answers should mention the formation and structure of the Iroquois League, particularly the power awarded to a Great Council to decide matters of great importance.

Indians of the Plains and Northwest Coast

Directions Complete this graphic organizer to compare and contrast the Indians of the Plains and the Indians of the Northwest Coast.

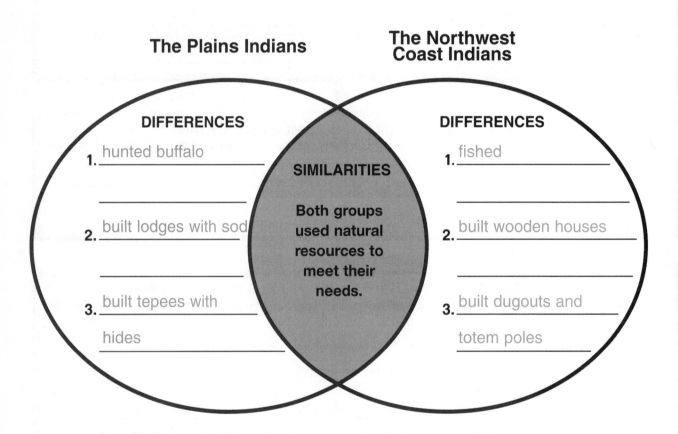

The Plains Indians

The Northwest Coast Indians

DIFFERENCES

1. hunted buffalo _____

_____

2. built lodges with sod _____

_____

3. built tepees with _____

hides _____

SIMILARITIES

Both groups used natural resources to meet their needs.

DIFFERENCES

1. fished _____

_____

2. built wooden houses _____

_____

3. built dugouts and _____

totem poles _____

2 Test Preparation

Directions Read each question and choose the best answer. Then fill in the circle for the answer you have chosen. Be sure to fill in the circle completely.

1 Which of the following explains early settlement in the Americas?
  Ⓐ land-bridge theory
  Ⓑ early-arrival theory
  Ⓒ origin stories
  ● all of the above

2 Which of the following shows the correct order of the development of civilizations in the Americas?
  Ⓕ the Olmecs, the Maya, the Mound Builders, the Anasazi
  ● the Olmecs, the Mound Builders, the Maya, the Anasazi
  Ⓗ the Maya, the Olmecs, the Mound Builders, the Anasazi
  Ⓙ the Olmecs, the Maya, the Anasazi, the Mound Builders

3 Which statement **best** describes the people of the Desert Southwest?
  ● They adapted their ways of life to fit their environment.
  Ⓑ They believed in gods of the sun, rain, and Earth.
  Ⓒ They lived in dome-shaped shelters called hogans.
  Ⓓ They shared certain customs.

4 Unlike the Northwest Coast Indians, the Arctic Indians—
  ● used animals for most of their food, shelter, and tools.
  Ⓖ lived in villages.
  Ⓗ hunted whales.
  Ⓙ raised their food on farms.

5 The Iroquois League—
  Ⓐ was a confederation made up of the Five Nations.
  Ⓑ relied on a Great Council to make important decisions.
  Ⓒ put an end to most Iroquois fighting.
  ● all of the above.

The World in the 1400s

Directions Use words and phrases from the Word Bank to complete the chart.

Aztecs	Mali	Ghana	Renaissance	Lake Texcoco
Portugal	Timbuktu	quipus	Vijayanagar	Songhay Empire
Cuzco	Incas	Zheng He	carved ivory	Johannes Gutenberg
compass	China	Benin	the Bible	Andes Mountains
junks				

The Americas	Europe	Asia	Africa
Aztecs	the Bible	junks	Ghana
Incas	Portugal	China	Timbuktu
Cuzco	Renaissance	Zheng He	Mali
quipus	Johannes Gutenberg	Vijayanagar	Songhay Empire
Andes Mountains		compass	Benin
Lake Texcoco			carved ivory

Directions Write your answer to each question.

1 In what ways did the peoples of the Americas, Europe, Asia, and Africa interact with one another in the 1400s? The peoples of these lands interacted by exploration and trade.

_____

2 How did China change after the death of its ruler Yong Le?
Yong Le encouraged exploration of other lands; the new rulers decided to stop all voyages and keep China apart from other civilizations.

_____

Use after reading Chapter 3, Lesson 1, pages 106–111.

Name _____ Date _____

MAP AND GLOBE SKILLS
Follow Routes on a Map

The Chinese Emperor sent admiral Zheng He, an explorer, on several voyages to explore the oceans surrounding China. From 1405 to 1433, Zheng He's fleets sailed on at least seven voyages. The admiral and his crew used wooden sailing ships called junks. The junks had flat bottoms, high masts, and square sails. Zheng He's expeditions took him to trading centers along the coast of China, as well as to the cities of Majapahit, Calicut, Hormuz, Mecca, and Mogadishu.

Directions Use the map to help you answer the questions.

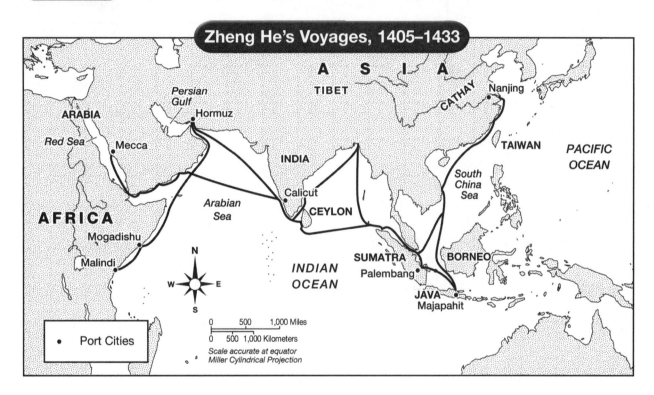

1. In what country is Calicut located? India

2. Zheng He started his voyages in Cathay, or China. In which directions did he travel to reach Hormuz? south, then northwest

3. In what direction did Zheng He travel to get from Hormuz to Mogadishu?

southwest

4. What city in Arabia did Zheng He visit? Mecca

Name _____ Date _____

Background to European Exploration

Directions Use the map and key to help you answer the questions. Write your answers in the blanks provided.

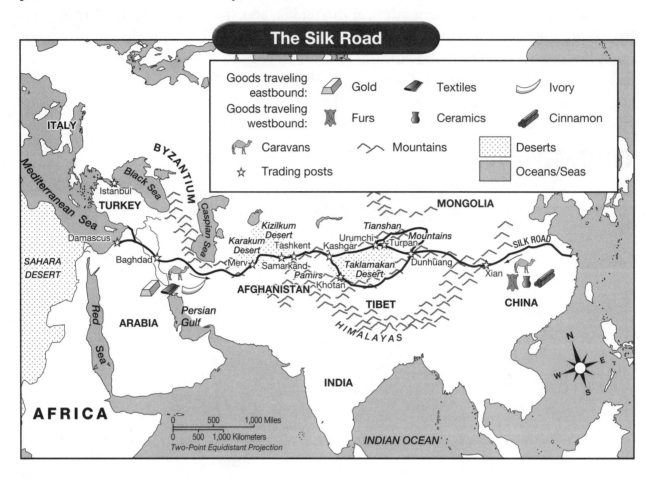

1 What are three kinds of goods transported by caravans traveling west through the Taklamakan Desert?

_____furs_____, _____ceramics_____, _____cinnamon_____

2 What three kinds of terrain would a caravan cross when traveling from Istanbul to Xian?

_____water_____, _____mountains_____, _____desert_____

3 What three deserts are along the Silk Road?

_____Kizilkum_____, _____Taklamakan_____, _____Karakum_____

Use after reading Chapter 3, Lesson 2, pages 114–119.

Name _____ Date _____

READING SKILLS

Identify Causes and Their Effects

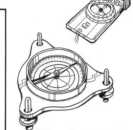

Directions Write the cause for each effect in the box provided.

Emperor Sunni Aui comes to power	development of the astrolabe	development of the caravel
invention of the compass	Turks capture Constantinople	cartographers begin working together
expeditions	Silk Road	

The compass—ancient and modern

CAUSE	→	EFFECT

CAUSE		**EFFECT**
expeditions		**enabled explorers to discover new lands and established routes for future explorations**
Turks capture Constantinople		**closed the Silk Road, stopping trade between Europe and Asia**
development of the caravel		**enabled explorers and merchants to travel long distances at a faster speed while carrying more cargo; led to more extended ocean exploration**
invention of the compass		**navigational tool that allowed longer voyages and more accurate sailing**
Silk Road		**enabled Europeans to travel over land to Asian trade cities**
cartographers begin working together		**improved navigation by making more accurate maps**
development of the astrolabe		**improved navigation by helping sailors use the position of the sun or the North Star to find their location**

Name _____ Date _____

Europeans Reach the Americas

Directions Complete the chart using the information in the Word Bank. Some pieces of information may be used more than once.

Columbus

Home Country	Planned Destination	Expedition Date	Importance of Exploration
Italy	Asia	1497	He was the first explorer to prove Vespucci's idea.
Portugal	Cathay	1499	The king of England sent him to find great riches.
Spain	The Isthmus of Panama	1500	He claimed Brazil for Portugal.
		1513	He realized that he and other explorers had found an unknown continent.
		1522	His attempt to find a western route to Asia led the Europeans to the Americas.

Explorer	Home Country	Planned Destination	Expedition Date	Importance of Exploration
Columbus	Italy	Asia	1492	His attempt to find a western route to Asia led the Europeans to the Americas.
Caboto	Italy	Cathay	1497	The king of England sent him to find great riches.
Magellan	Spain	Asia	1522	He was the first explorer to sail around the world.
Vespucci	Italy	Asia	1499	He realized that he and other explorers had found an unknown continent.
Balboa	Spain	The Isthmus of Panama	1513	He was the first explorer to prove Vespucci's idea.
Cabral	Portugal	Brazil	1500	He claimed Brazil for Portugal.

Use after reading Chapter 3, Lesson 3, pages 121–126.

The Spanish Conquerors

Ponce de León

Directions Write "T" or "F" in the blank before each statement to tell whether it is **TRUE** or **FALSE**. If the statement is **FALSE**, write the word that would make it **TRUE** in the blank at the end of the statement.

___F___ **1** The <u>English</u> king offered grants of money to explorers who would lead expeditions. <u>Spanish_____</u>

___T___ **2** In 1513 Ponce de León set out to find <u>Bimini</u> and the "Fountain of Youth." _____

___F___ **3** Ponce de León claimed the land now known as Florida and named it *La Florida*, which is Spanish for "<u>conquer.</u>" <u>"flowery"_____</u>

___F___ **4** Cortés had heard stories about the great wealth of the <u>Inca</u> Empire. <u>Aztec_____</u>

___T___ **5** In 1519 Cortés traveled from the tropical coast to the Valley of Mexico, finally reaching <u>Tenochtitlán</u>. _____

___F___ **6** The <u>French</u> who were unhappy with Aztec rule gave the Spanish food and support against the Aztecs. <u>Native Americans_____</u>

___T___ **7** The Aztec people believed that Cortés might be <u>Quetzalcoatl</u>. _____

___F___ **8** The survivors of Narváez's expedition sailed along the <u>Pacific Coast</u> until they reached Spanish lands in Mexico. <u>Gulf Coast_____</u>

___F___ **9** Coronado and several Spaniards, Africans, and Native Americans set out to find the Seven Cities of <u>Steel</u>. <u>Gold_____</u>

___F___ **10** In 1539 Hernando de Soto explored much of the North American <u>Northwest</u>. <u>Southeast_____</u>

Search for the Northwest Passage

Directions Use the Word Bank below to complete the sentences.

Arctic Ocean	Northwest Passage	estuary	*Half Moon*
gold	Iroquois	Dutch East India Company	*Dauphine*
King Francis I	Staten Island		Pamlico Sound

1 European explorers were looking for the _____ Northwest Passage _____ , a waterway along the north coast of North America connecting the Atlantic Ocean and the Pacific Ocean.

2 In 1524 Giovanni da Verrazano set sail for North America

on his ship, the _____ *Dauphine* _____ .

Verrazano

3 A narrow body of water called the _____ Pamlico Sound _____ lay between the Atlantic Ocean and what Verrazano thought was the Pacific Ocean.

4 Verrazano landed on the north end of present-day

_____ Staten Island _____ .

Cartier

5 _____ King Francis I _____ sent Jacques Cartier

to North America to search for _____ gold _____ and other valuable metals.

6 Cartier's ship sailed up the _____ estuary _____ of the St. Lawrence River.

7 During his expedition, Cartier was told by the _____ Iroquois _____ of jewels and metals that could be found northwest of Gaspe Peninsula.

8 Henry Hudson sailed by way of the _____ Arctic Ocean _____ in search of the Northwest Passage.

9 The _____ Dutch East India Company _____ gave Hudson a ship for his third voyage, his last attempt to find the Northwest Passage.

Hudson

10 Hudson's crew aboard the _____ *Half Moon* _____ mutinied in 1609.

Use after reading Chapter 3, Lesson 5, pages 136–139.

European Exploration

Directions Complete this graphic organizer to show that you understand the causes and effects of some of the key events that encouraged exploration and led to the discovery of the Americas.

CAUSE	EFFECT	EFFECT
Columbus gets King Ferdinand and Queen Isabella to support his expedition.	Columbus is able to sail west with 89 sailors and three ships.	**Columbus lands at San Salvador.**

CAUSE	EFFECT	EFFECT
De Soto and an army of 600 soldiers sail to the west coast of Florida in search of gold.	In their unsuccessful three-year search for gold, de Soto and his army explore all of what is today the southeastern United States.	**The Spanish claim all of what is today the southeastern United States.**

3

Test Preparation

Directions Read each question and choose the best answer. Then fill in the circle for the answer you have chosen. Be sure to fill in the circle completely.

1 Many years before Europeans arrived in the Americas, some groups of Native Americans had established powerful—
- Ⓐ tribes.
- Ⓑ fleets of ships.
- Ⓒ empires.
- Ⓓ trade agreements with China.

2 A compass and an astrolabe are kinds of _____ sailors used to determine their location at sea.
- Ⓕ construction tools
- Ⓖ navigational tools
- Ⓗ books
- Ⓙ telescopes

3 When Columbus landed in the Americas, he thought he was in _____.
- Ⓐ Asia
- Ⓑ Spain
- Ⓒ Mexico
- Ⓓ Portugal

4 The Portuguese explorer _____ was the first to sail around the world.
- Ⓕ Columbus
- Ⓖ Magellan
- Ⓗ Vespucci
- Ⓙ Cabral

5 King Francis I was one of many European rulers who wanted to find the _____ through North America.
- Ⓐ Santa Fe Trail
- Ⓑ Silk Road
- Ⓒ trade route
- Ⓓ Northwest Passage

New Spain

Directions Write the number of the sentence under the appropriate heading in the Venn diagram.

Before Spanish Colonies Established	Before and After	After Spanish Colonies Established
3, 7, 8	4, 9	1, 2, 5, 6, 10

1 Many Native Americans died from a disease called smallpox.

2 The Plains Indians tamed horses and used them for hunting.

3 Native Americans were free from European diseases.

4 Gold, silver, and other treasures could be found in North America.

5 Native American tribes living in the borderlands traded with the Spanish.

6 The Navajos raised sheep and wove the wool into colorful clothing and blankets.

7 People could not travel on the *El Camino Real.*

8 Many Native Americans lived as free peoples in what is today known as Mexico.

9 Many Native Americans followed their traditional religions.

10 Missionaries persuaded some Native Americans to become Catholics.

Name _____ Date _____

New France

Directions Fill in the missing information in this letter from a member of Louis Joliet's crew. Use the words below to help you complete the letter.

Jacques Marquette	Lake Michigan	Indian	canoes	1673
Northwest Passage	Mississippi	Spanish	languages	south

Dear Family:

In this year of ___1673___, I think of you often. I have set out with Joliet's crew on an expedition to find a great river called the ___Mississippi___. We are traveling with a missionary named ___Jacques Marquette___ who speaks many Indian ___languages___.

We started our journey from northern ___Lake Michigan___ in birch-bark ___canoes___. We crossed a huge lake and several rivers. At last we saw the great Mississippi! Unfortunately, we realized it was not the ___Northwest Passage___ that we were looking for because it flows ___south___.

When we reached the mouth of the Arkansas River, we met some ___Indian___ people who told us of Europeans living farther South along the river. We think those Europeans might be the ___Spanish___. We fear they may attack us, so we have decided to turn back.

I will think of you all as I journey home.

Sincerely,
François

The English in the Americas

Directions Some of these sentences are causes, and some are effects.
Complete the chart to show each cause and its effect.

> "Sea dogs" like Francis Drake become pirates.
>
> Treasure captured by "sea dogs" helps increase England's wealth.
>
> England decides to start colonies in America.
>
> The English colonists at Roanoke Island arrive too late in the year to plant crops.

CAUSE → **EFFECT**

CAUSE	EFFECT
Elizabeth I encourages English sea captains to attack Spanish treasure ships.	"Sea dogs" like Francis Drake become pirates.
Treasure captured by "sea dogs" helps increase England's wealth.	England builds a strong navy with that wealth and becomes a powerful country.
Europe's most powerful countries have colonies in America.	England decides to start colonies in America.
The English colonists at Roanoke Island arrive too late in the year to plant crops.	John White returns to England to gather food and supplies.

Name ______________________ Date ______________

The Jamestown Colony

Directions **Use the chart below to answer the questions that follow.**

House of Burgesses			
Who?	**What?**	**When or Where?**	**How?**
Each Virginia settlement or plantation was allowed to elect two burgesses, usually wealthy landowners.	Virginia's legislature, the branch of the government that makes laws	Established July 30, 1619	Burgesses would meet once a year with the royal governor.
The 22 original burgesses were members of the House of Burgesses.	The first lawmaking assembly formed in the English colonies	Jamestown Colony	Burgesses and royal governor would meet to make local laws and decide on taxes.
Royal Governor George Yeardley shared ruling authority with the House of Burgesses.	Jamestown Colony would live under English law and have the same rights as the people living in England.	Met in the Jamestown church	Modeled after the English Parliament

1. What did the House of Burgesses do? They made laws for the Virginia Colony.

2. What country ruled Jamestown? England

3. Who was the royal governor? George Yeardley

4. How often did the royal governor meet with the burgesses?
   once a year

5. What governing body was the House of Burgesses modeled after?
   the English Parliament

6. When was the House of Burgesses established? July 30, 1619

7. How did the burgesses decide on laws and taxes? They met with the royal governor.

8. How many burgesses could be elected from each plantation or settlement?
   2

Use after reading Chapter 4, Lesson 4, pages 160–164.

Name _____ Date _____

CITIZENSHIP SKILLS
Solve a Problem

Directions One problem in colonial times was that of getting settlers to stay for long periods of time. Imagine that you are a leader who wants to settle a colony. Use the steps below to complete the boxes and help you solve the problem. Step 1 has been done for you.

Here are some questions to think about when solving your problem:

Where will the colonists live? How will they get food? How will they make a living? How will they prepare for winter? Who will govern the settlements? How will they respond to conflicts with other people?

Step 1 Identify the problem.	Step 2 Gather information about the problem.	Step 3 Think of and list possible options.
People are not permanently settling in the colonies.	Step 2 should include reasons that colonists are not remaining, such as illness, starvation, conflicts with Native Americans, poor farming, not enough supplies.	Step 3 should include ways to meet these challenges, such as moving to areas that offer better farming, training people to farm the land, storing enough food to get them through the winter.

Step 4 Consider the advantages and disadvantages of possible options.	Step 5 Choose the best solution.	Step 6 Try your solution.	Step 7 Think about how well your solution helps solve the problem.
Step 4 should offer advantages and disadvantages for each option: example—another area is better for farming but is occupied by Native Americans.	Step 5 should name the solution the student chooses to fix the problem, for example, teach colonists to survive with the skills they have.	Step 6 should explain how the solution would be applied to the problem.	Step 7 should list how the plan could work and reasons why it might not work.

The Plymouth Colony

Directions When the Mayflower Compact was written in 1620, the English language was very different from what it is today. Below is a version of the Mayflower Compact written in present-day language. Use it to answer the questions that follow.

The Mayflower Compact

In the name of God, Amen. We, the loyal subjects of King James and the people of God have taken a voyage to settle in the first colony in the northern parts of Virginia. We, the people whose names are signed below, have made an agreement, in the presence of God and one another, to establish our own government of fair and equal laws. These laws will be decided by the majority rule of this group. These laws are made for the good of the people in the colony as well as for the colony itself. We promise to obey the laws we have made. We have signed our names below, at Cape Cod, on November 11, 1620.

Myles Standish   *William Bradford*

1 Who is the English ruler named in the Mayflower Compact?

King James

2 Where did the Mayflower passengers think they were going to settle?

the northern parts of Virginia

3 How did the writers of the Mayflower Compact say laws would be decided?

They would be decided by majority rule.

4 What did the passengers promise? to obey the laws they made

5 Where and when was the Mayflower Compact signed? _____

Cape Cod; November 11, 1620

Name _____ Date _____

Compare Tables to Classify Information

Directions Read and study each table. Use the information in the tables to answer the questions below.

Table A: Native Americans and European Colonists		
Colony	**Native American Tribe Encountered**	**Interaction/Events**
Connecticut (1636)	Pequot	Colonists purchased land; later, tribe fought to reclaim land.
New Jersey (1664)	Lenape	Colonists fought with this hostile tribe.
New York (1626)	Algonquian-speaking tribes	Colonists bought Manhattan Island from local tribes.
Rhode Island (1636)	Algonquian-speaking tribes, mostly Narragansett	Colonists peacefully coexisted with local tribes.

Table B: Native Americans and European Colonists		
Interaction/Events	**Native American Tribe Encountered**	**Colony**
Colonists bought Manhattan Island from local tribes.	Algonquian-speaking tribes	New York (1626)
Colonists purchased land; later, tribe fought to reclaim land.	Pequot	Connecticut (1636)
Colonists peacefully coexisted with local tribes.	Algonquian-speaking tribes, mostly Narragansett	Rhode Island (1636)
Colonists fought with this hostile tribe.	Lenape	New Jersey (1664)

1 Which table makes it easier to find out when the first colony was established?

Why? Table B; the Colony column is in date order.

2 Which table would you use to find which colony bought an island from Native

Americans? Why? Table B; the interaction is in the first column.

3 Which table would you use to find out which Native American tribe was found

in New Jersey? Why? Table A; states listed are in the first column.

Key Settlements in North America

Directions Complete this graphic organizer by categorizing people and settlements with the country they are associated with.

SPANISH SETTLEMENTS	FRENCH SETTLEMENTS	ENGLISH SETTLEMENTS

SPANISH SETTLEMENTS

KEY PEOPLE

1. **Bartolomé de Las Casas**

2. Pedro Menéndez de Avilés

3. Junípero Serra

_____

KEY SETTLEMENTS

1. **Hispaniola**

2. Castillo de San Marcos

3. Nombre de Dios

_____

_____

FRENCH SETTLEMENTS

KEY PEOPLE

1. **Samuel de Champlain**

2. Count de Frontenac

3. Pierre LeMoyne/Jean Baptiste LeMoyne

KEY SETTLEMENTS

1. **Quebec**

2. St. Louis, Des Moines

3. New Orleans

_____

_____

ENGLISH SETTLEMENTS

KEY PEOPLE

1. **Sir Francis Drake**

2. Sir Walter Raleigh

3. John White

_____

KEY SETTLEMENTS

1. **Roanoke**

2. Jamestown

3. Plymouth Colony

_____

_____

Name _____ Date _____

4 Test Preparation

Directions Read each question and choose the best answer. Then fill in the circle for the answer you have chosen. Be sure to fill in the circle completely.

1 What did the Spanish create in North America to protect their colonies from other Europeans?
- (A) a hacienda
- (B) a buffer zone
- (C) a mission
- (D) a ranch

2 What was the main item of trade between the French and the Native Americans in New France?
- (F) fur
- (G) gold
- (H) silk
- (J) food

3 Who protected the English "sea dogs" when they stole treasures from the Spanish?
- (A) Native Americans
- (B) the French
- (C) the queen of England
- (D) conquistadors

4 What is a burgess?
- (F) a representative
- (G) a royal governor
- (H) a company
- (J) a monarchy

5 Why did the Pilgrims sail to North America in 1620?
- (A) to meet Native Americans
- (B) to practice their religion in their own way
- (C) to be farmers
- (D) to trade fur

Massachusetts Bay Colony

Directions Find the terms in the Word Bank in the Word Search Puzzle.
Words may be arranged vertically, horizontally, or diagonally.

Puritan	charter	common	specialize	town meeting
public office	blacksmith	churn	colony	confederation
school	constable	kettle	patchwork quilts	candles
livestock	soap	crops	preserved	pickled vegetables

```
y s d e h c s o o c v d c a n d l e s b q z s d f w q
h k o f d e s n a h r t e d f h j c c o l o n y u b t
n r v y q w p p r e s e r v e d a o y k a n b m k g b
y t r d c t d e a m c b n t i u u d h p c p x v c s l
t j u u o r d c e t o w n m e e t i n g a u a k r f a
n m t l n o l u p i c k l e d v e g e t a b l e s q c
k g f t s e d t u y h h j k g o y t g b j l s f d a k
d e i b t u y t r c a x w l k u j h v y u i c z i x s
c r t v a b c n i l r v c o m m o n y a o c r m x u m
b t f t b j h k t v t x h d r l k i j d c o k s d s i
i u f r l h z s a r e g u g m k g h r f y f e r p c t
w s b n e e k m n y r e r s d e q j f w d f j o d h h
o l p u h j f r t d o k n f d e t u i u y i r x c o m
w d e s s p e c i a l i z e t f h y i r e c i u k o p
u e h s g a i w k e d j o l h j i k g l t e c w o l n
k l n f l i v e s t o c k d a s j w e h t a g n c b d
m f d j s e i c o n f e d e r a t i o n k s s a e l s
```

(continued)

Use after reading Chapter 5, Lesson 1, pages 188–193.

Name _____ Date _____

Directions Use words from the word bank on the previous page to complete the sentences below.

1 In 1628 King Charles I granted a _____ charter _____,

to a group of Puritans, allowing them to settle in New England.

2 John Winthrop served as governor in one _____ colony _____ several times during a 20-year period.

3 Winthrop formed a _____ confederation _____ among the people of New England so they could better defend themselves against their enemies.

4 A place for the town animals to graze was one use for the

_____ common _____.

5 A _____ blacksmith _____ specialized in working with iron.

6 A law was passed stating that any town with more than 50 families must

have a _____ school _____.

7 Both men and women could attend a _____ town meeting _____, but only the men could vote.

8 One public official was a _____ constable _____, who was in charge of maintaining order and keeping the peace.

9 _____ Pickled vegetables _____ could be stored and eaten throughout the winter.

10 Some food, as well as leather and wool, came from farmers'

_____ livestock _____.

New Ideas, New Colonies

Directions Complete the information in the boxes next to the map. Use the names and terms below to help you.

Thomas Hooker	Roger Williams	consent
John Endecott	Fundamental Orders	self-governed by Puritan leaders

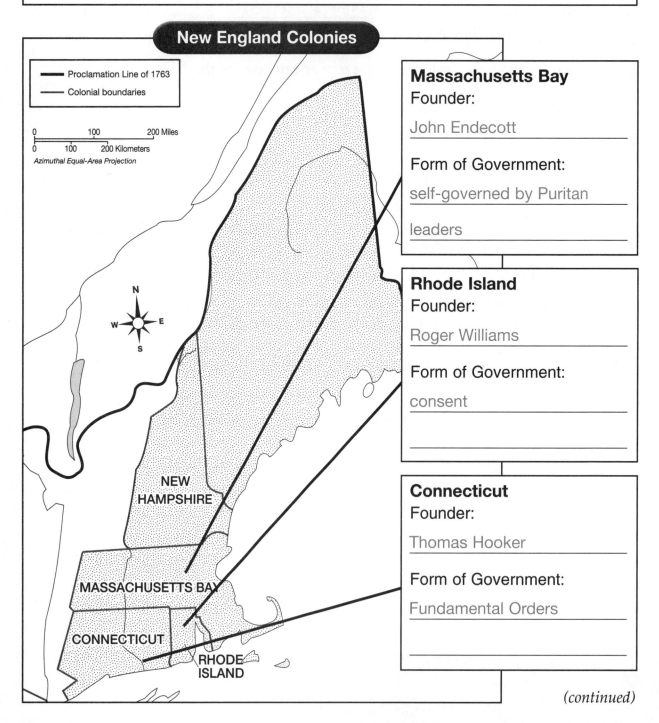

New England Colonies

Proclamation Line of 1763
Colonial boundaries

0   100   200 Miles
0   100   200 Kilometers
Azimuthal Equal-Area Projection

NEW HAMPSHIRE

MASSACHUSETTS BAY

CONNECTICUT

RHODE ISLAND

Massachusetts Bay
Founder:
John Endecott

Form of Government:
self-governed by Puritan
leaders

Rhode Island
Founder:
Roger Williams

Form of Government:
consent

Connecticut
Founder:
Thomas Hooker

Form of Government:
Fundamental Orders

(continued)

Name _____ Date _____

Directions Use the map on the previous page and the words and sentences below to help you complete the table and answer the questions.

Places, Tribes, and Dates:	Events:
1636	Expelled from the colony, Williams moved his family to Narragansett Bay.
Narragansett	
Windsor, 1633	Puritans disagreed with practices of the Church of England.
Providence, 1636	

Founded	Massachusetts Bay Colony	Rhode Island Colony	Connecticut Colony
When	1628	1636	1630s
Why	Puritans disagreed with practices of the Church of England.	Expelled from the colony, Williams moved his family to Narragansett Bay.	Some colonists were looking for better farmland; other colonists wanted religious freedom.
Where	Salem, 1628	Providence, 1636	Windsor, 1633
Which tribe was there?	Wampanoags	Narragansett	Pequots

❶ When was the Connecticut Colony founded? <u>1630s</u>

❷ What was the major event that led to the founding of the Massachusetts Bay Colony? <u>Puritans disagreed with practices of the Church of England.</u>

❸ What Native American tribe did the Massachusetts Bay Colony interact with?
<u>Wampanoags</u>

❹ Who moved to Narragansett Bay? <u>Roger Williams</u>

New England's Economy

Coastal Industries of Colonial New England

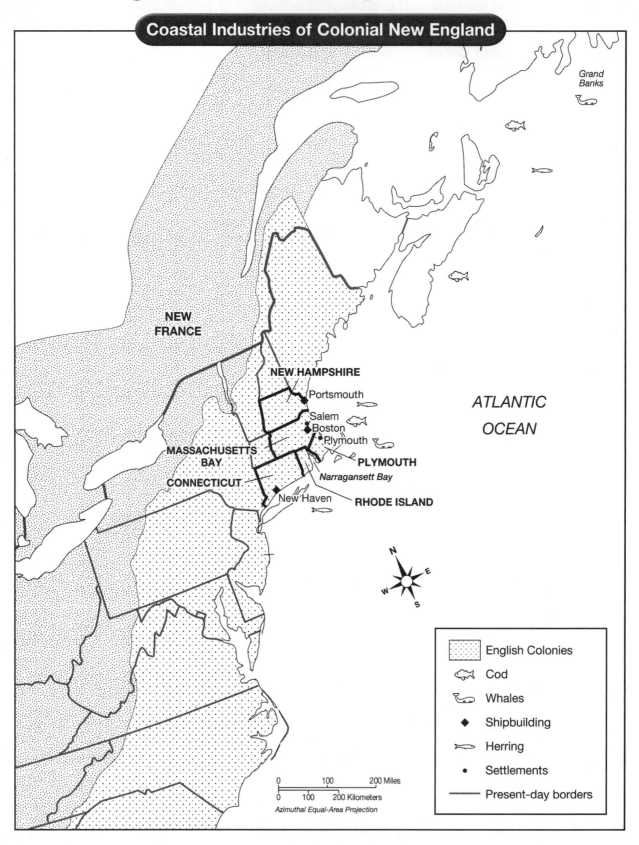

(continued)

Use after reading Chapter 5, Lesson 3, pages 200–204.

Name _____ Date _____

Directions Use the map on page 48 to help you answer some of the questions below.

1 Shade in the area that shows the New England Colonies.

2 Other than the English colonies, what land area was near the Grand Banks?

New France

3 In what three settlements and colonies were the shipbuilding centers located?

Portsmouth, New Hampshire; Boston, Massachusetts Bay; New Haven,

Connecticut

4 What were two locations where whales were caught? near Plymouth and in
the Grand Banks

5 In what ocean did the colonists fish? Atlantic Ocean

6 What important product came from whales, and what was it used for?

Whale fat, or blubber; it was used to make oil for lamps.

7 When whalers first began hunting, they used small rowboats and were able to find many whales near the shore. Later, the whalers needed bigger ships, and their whaling trips lasted much longer. Sometimes, whalers were gone for many months or even years. Explain why the whaling industry changed.

At first, there were many whales along the coast. Then, as more whalers

began hunting, the whale population decreased, so whalers had to travel

longer distances to find whales and were gone longer.

8 Why did shipbuilders choose coastal locations such as Portsmouth for

shipbuilding? They needed to be near the ocean to sail the ships and near

the forest to get the wood they needed. It was also much cheaper to

build ships in the colonies than to buy ships from England.

CHART AND GRAPH SKILLS
Use a Line Graph

Directions Study the line graph below. Use it to help you determine whether the statements on page 51 are true or false.

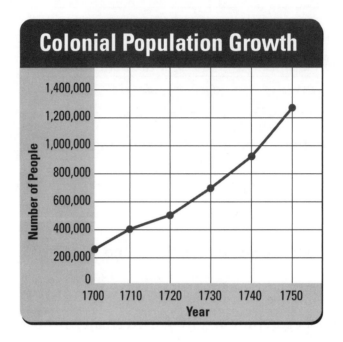

Colonial Population Growth

Directions Circle *T* if the sentence is true. Circle *F* if the sentence is false.

1 There were more than 2 million people in the colonies by 1750. T (F)

2 The population growth was less than 500,000 between 1700 and 1710. (T) F

3 There were nearly twice as many people in 1740 as there were in 1720. (T) F

4 One of the largest population increases occurred between 1720 and 1730. T (F)

(continued)

Use after reading Chapter 5, Skill Lesson, page 205.

5 The population was almost a million people in 1740.   (T)   F

6 Given the growth of the population between 1740 and 1750, what would the projected population be for 1760? Read the graph, and list the numbers for each point on the graph.

1740 _about 920,000_____

1750 _about 1,250,000_____

1760 _about 1,580,000_____

7 By the early 1700s the colonies were well established and colonists were relatively healthy. Many colonists had large families—sometimes with ten or more children. In addition, new settlers continued to arrive. Using the line graph, explain the effect that these factors had on the population of the colonies.

The population of the colonies continued to grow.

_____

_____

The Massachusetts Bay Colony

Directions Complete this graphic organizer by summarizing the following facts about the Massachusetts Bay Colony.

FACTS		SUMMARY

1. The Puritans built many villages in North America. 2. The most important building in a Puritan village was the meetinghouse. 3. The village meetinghouse served as a church and a place to hold town meetings.		In Puritan villages the most important building was the meetinghouse, which served as both a church and a place to hold town meetings.
1. Roger Williams was forced to leave the Massachusetts Bay Colony. 2. Anne Hutchinson was also forced to leave the colony. 3. Roger Williams and Anne Hutchinson and their followers established their own settlements.		Forced to leave the Massachusetts Bay Colony, both Roger Williams and Anne Hutchinson established their own settlements.
1. Trading goods made many people wealthy in New England. 2. Goods were traded between the colonies, England, and the west coast of Africa. 3. Trade brought the first African slaves to the English Colonies.		Though trade made many people in New England wealthy, it also brought the first African slaves to the English Colonies.

Use after reading Chapter 5, pages 187–205.

Name _____ Date _____

5 Test Preparation

Directions Read each question and choose the best answer. Then fill in the circle for the answer you have chosen. Be sure to fill in the circle completely.

1 Which group of people settled in New England because they disagreed with many practices of the Church of England?
- Ⓐ colonists
- Ⓑ settlers
- Ⓒ Puritans ●
- Ⓓ Christians

2 Who had a conflict with the Puritan leaders in the Massachusetts Bay Colony?
- Ⓕ Anne Hutchinson
- Ⓖ Roger Williams
- Ⓗ both F and G ●
- Ⓙ John Winthrop

3 Where did some colonists go to find better farmland?
- Ⓐ Rhode Island
- Ⓑ Connecticut ●
- Ⓒ Massachusetts Bay
- Ⓓ Plymouth

4 Why was whale oil a popular product?
- Ⓕ It burned brightly without an unpleasant odor. ●
- Ⓖ It was very inexpensive.
- Ⓗ It was available in unlimited quantities.
- Ⓙ both G and H

5 _____ were workers who used wood to make barrels and casks.
- Ⓐ Merchants
- Ⓑ Shipbuilders
- Ⓒ Fishermen
- Ⓓ Coopers ●

Breadbasket Colonies

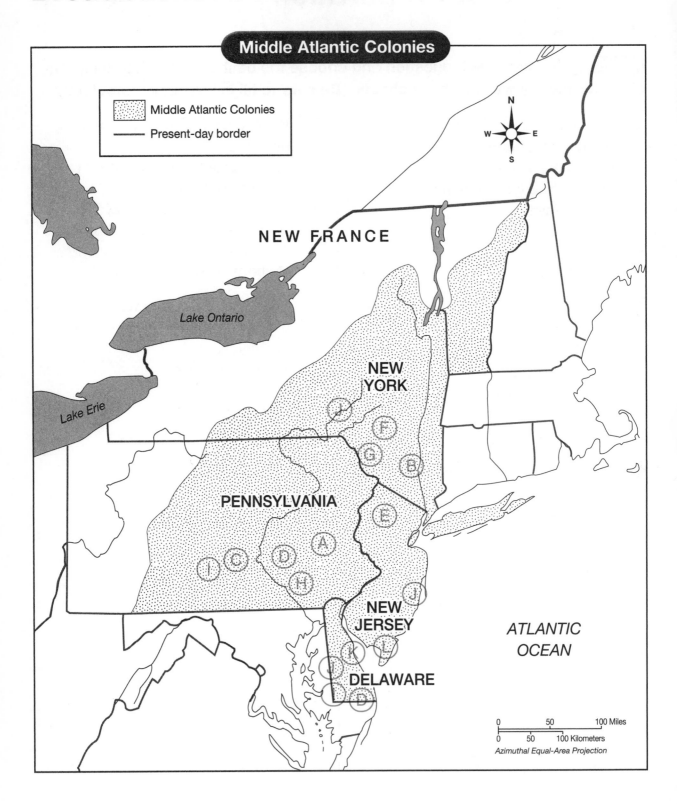

Middle Atlantic Colonies

Legend:
- Middle Atlantic Colonies
- Present-day border

NEW FRANCE

Lake Ontario

Lake Erie

NEW YORK

PENNSYLVANIA

NEW JERSEY

DELAWARE

ATLANTIC OCEAN

0   50   100 Miles
0   50   100 Kilometers
Azimuthal Equal-Area Projection

(continued)

Use after reading Chapter 6, Lesson 1, pages 210–215.

Directions Read each lettered phrase below. On the map, write the letter of the phrase in the colony or colonies to which it applies.

A. settled by Quakers Pennsylvania

B. bought from the Manhattan Indians by Peter Minuit New York

C. freedom of speech, freedom of worship, and trial by jury Pennsylvania

D. William Penn Pennsylvania and Delaware

E. John Berkeley and George Carteret New Jersey

F. colonists fought Delaware and Wappinger Indians New York

G. Peter Stuyvesant New York

H. "Penn's woods" Pennsylvania

I. Native American Chief Tamenend Pennsylvania and Delaware

J. claimed for Holland by Henry Hudson New York, New Jersey, and Delaware

K. Fort Christina Delaware

L. Edward Byllinge New Jersey

Why were the Middle Atlantic Colonies called the "breadbasket colonies"?

The Middle Atlantic Colonies were called the "breadbasket colonies" because they

produced many crops used in the making of bread, such as wheat, corn, and rye.

_____

_____

_____

_____

_____

_____

_____

Colonial Philadelphia

Benjamin Franklin

William Penn

Facts About William Penn and Benjamin Franklin

Founded Philadelphia on the idea that people of different backgrounds could live in peace together

Wrote "Early to bed and early to rise makes a man healthy, wealthy, and wise"

Designed the layout of Philadelphia, with a "checkerboard" plan for the center

Printed a newspaper called the *Pennsylvania Gazette*

Organized the first firefighting company in the colonies

Named his colony's chief city Philadelphia

Worked to have Philadelphia's streets lit at night and paved

Divided his colony into townships made up of 5,000 acres each

Helped establish the first subscription library

Added public parks to the city he called "a green country town"

Planned the government and the settlements of Philadelphia

Invented the lightning rod, which helped protect buildings from lightning

(continued)

Name _____ Date _____

Directions Read the facts about William Penn and Benjamin Franklin on page 56. Decide which facts describe each person. Then use the facts to fill in the table below.

William Penn	Benjamin Franklin
Named his colony's chief city Philadelphia	Organized the first firefighting company in the colonies
Planned the government and the settlements of Philadelphia	Worked to have Philadelphia's streets lit at night and paved
Added public parks to the city he called "a green country town"	Helped establish the first subscription library
Founded Philadelphia on the idea that people of different backgrounds could live in peace together	Invented the lightning rod, which helped protect buildings from lightning
Divided his colony into townships made up of 5,000 acres each	Printed a newspaper called the *Pennsylvania Gazette*
Designed the layout of Philadelphia, with a "checkerboard" plan for the center	Wrote "Early to bed and early to rise makes a man healthy, wealthy, and wise"

CHART AND GRAPH SKILLS
Use a Circle Graph

Directions Use the circle graph to help you answer the questions below.

Population of the 13 Colonies, 1750

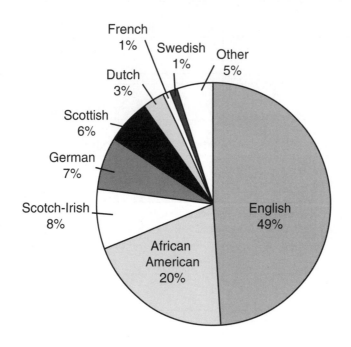

① What was the largest ethnic group in the 13 colonies in 1750?

English

② What were the smallest ethnic groups? Swedish and French

③ Which group was larger, German or Scottish? German

④ What percent of the population was African American? 20%

⑤ What was the combined percent of African American and English people?

69%

⑥ What was the combined percent of all non-English people?

51%

(continued)

Name _____ Date _____

Directions **Use the table to help you complete the activities.**

In addition to Quaker meetinghouses, there were many kinds of churches in Pennsylvania. Use the information in the table to make a circle graph of the kinds of churches in Pennsylvania other than Quaker meetinghouses.

Pennsylvania Churches* in 1750	
Church	**Percent of Population**
Dutch Reformed	32%
Lutheran	28%
Baptist	15%
Anglican	10%
German Reformed	6%
Catholic	6%
Congregationalist	3%

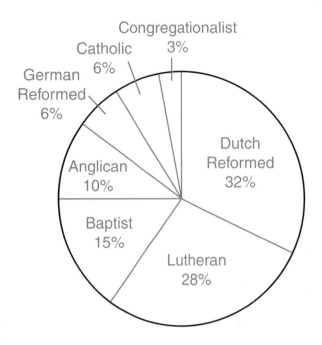

*Quaker meetinghouses not included

Use the information from the circle graph you have made to write a paragraph about church memberships in Pennsylvania. Be sure to discuss why you think Pennsylvania had so many different kinds of churches.

Answers will vary but should mention how most people in Pennsylvania attended

Dutch Reform or Lutheran churches. Students should also mention that

Pennsylvania's religious diversity was a result of William Penn's idea that people

of different backgrounds and religions could live in peace together.

_____

_____

_____

_____

Moving West

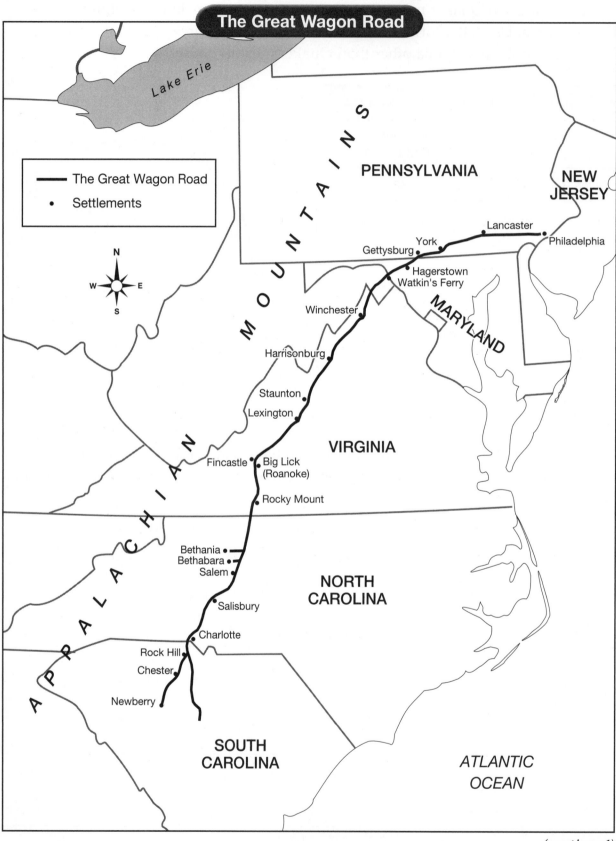

The Great Wagon Road

Lake Erie

PENNSYLVANIA

NEW JERSEY

The Great Wagon Road
Settlements

M O U N T A I N S

Lancaster
York
Gettysburg
Hagerstown
Watkin's Ferry
Philadelphia

MARYLAND

Winchester

Harrisonburg

Staunton
Lexington

VIRGINIA

A P P A L A C H I A N

Fincastle • Big Lick
(Roanoke)

Rocky Mount

Bethania
Bethabara
Salem

NORTH
CAROLINA

Salisbury

Charlotte
Rock Hill
Chester
Newberry

SOUTH
CAROLINA

ATLANTIC
OCEAN

(continued)

Use after reading Chapter 6, Lesson 3, pages 224–227.

Name _____ Date _____

Directions Read the paragraph below and use the map on the previous page to label the sentences. If the sentence is true, write *T* in the blank provided. If it is false, write *F*.

Traveling on the Great Wagon Road

The Great Wagon Road extended from Pennsylvania to South Carolina. Travel along the hilly route was difficult, and journeys lasted at least two months. Even the fastest wagon traveled only five miles a day. Often people crossed rivers by wading through them while guiding their wagons or carrying supplies. Although the weather was harsh, people frequently made the trip in winter because it was easier to travel on the frozen roads. Each year the Great Wagon Road stretched farther south, so that by 1775 it was close to 600 miles long. In the decade before the American Revolution, tens of thousands of settlers journeyed down the road in search of new opportunities. During this time, the Great Wagon Road was the most heavily traveled road in the colonies.

1 __F__ Settlements along the Great Wagon Road included York, Harrisonburg, Salisbury, and New York City.

2 __T__ Salisbury is located on the east side of the Great Wagon Road in North Carolina.

3 __T__ People frequently journeyed along the Great Wagon Road in the winter because it was easier to travel on the frozen roads.

4 __T__ The Great Wagon Road ran through parts of five different colonies.

5 __F__ The fastest wagons journeying on the Great Wagon Road traveled 25 miles a day.

6 Compare and contrast travel on American highways today with travel along the Great Wagon Road in the mid-1700s. Answers will vary. Students may mention their personal travel experiences and travel conditions compared to those of the Great Wagon Road.

_____

_____

_____

Name _____ Date _____

Chapter Review

Directions Complete this graphic organizer by using information you have learned from the chapter to make inferences about the Middle Atlantic Colonies and the backcountry.

Breadbasket Colonies

WHAT YOU HAVE READ	WHAT YOU KNOW
The Middle Atlantic Colonies attracted people from many different backgrounds.	Many people in your classroom or school are from different backgrounds.

The Middle Atlantic Colonies had a blend of many heritages.

_____

_____

Moving West

WHAT YOU HAVE READ	WHAT YOU KNOW
Colonists who settled land farther west faced many challenges.	Sometimes it can be difficult adjusting to new places and surroundings.

People who settled the West overcame these challenges and

successfully adjusted.

_____

Use after reading Chapter 6, pages 208–227.

6 Test Preparation

Directions Read each question and choose the best answer. Then fill in the circle for the answer you have chosen. Be sure to fill in the circle completely.

1 Farmers depended on _____ as places to trade their surplus farm produce.
- Ⓐ crops
- Ⓑ agriculture
- Ⓒ market towns
- Ⓓ meetinghouses

2 Philadelphia's location near good land and _____ was one reason it became Pennsylvania's main port.
- Ⓕ waterways
- Ⓖ wagon roads
- Ⓗ oceans
- Ⓙ fertile soil

3 The English and the _____ who came with William Penn were the largest groups of immigrants in Philadelphia.
- Ⓐ Puritans
- Ⓑ Catholics
- Ⓒ Quakers
- Ⓓ Shakers

4 The land between the Coastal Plain and the Appalachian Mountains is called the—
- Ⓕ farmland.
- Ⓖ backcountry.
- Ⓗ city.
- Ⓙ Fall Line.

5 Backcountry family members all had to do jobs or chores, such as—
- Ⓐ chopping wood.
- Ⓑ hunting.
- Ⓒ candle making.
- Ⓓ all of the above.

Settlement of the South

Directions Use the Word Bank to provide the missing information in the chart.

to make money from cash crops	Catholic landowners
the Lords Proprietors	James Oglethorpe
to give debtors a new start	French Huguenots
divided into two colonies	freedom to worship
1633	English

Settling the Southern Colonies			
Where	**Who**	**Why**	**When**
Maryland	Founders: the Calverts, Catholic landowners First proprietor: Cecilius Calvert First governor: Leonard Calvert	freedom to worship	1633
Carolina	First proprietors: the Lords Proprietors (8 English nobles) First colonists: English settlers, settlers from the Caribbean, and French Huguenots First governor: William Drummond	to make money from cash crops	1663 1712: divided into two colonies
Georgia	First proprietors: James Oglethorpe and 19 partners First colonists: English	to give debtors a new start	1733

(continued)

Use after reading Chapter 7, Lesson 1, pages 232–239.

Name _____ Date _____

Directions Use the chart on the preceding page to help you write answers to the questions.

1 Which colony wanted to help debtors? Georgia _____

2 What happened in Carolina in 1712? It divided into two colonies, North and

South Carolina. _____

3 Who were the Calverts? What colony did they found?

Catholic landowners; Maryland Colony _____

4 What freedom did the colonists of Maryland want? freedom to worship _____

_____

5 Who were the Lords Proprietors, and what was their role in the colony?

8 English nobles who governed the Carolina Colony. _____

6 From what country were the Huguenots? France _____

7 What colony grew cash crops? Why do you think cash crops were important to

the colonists? Carolina; Possible answer: They provided the colonies with money

and allowed them to prosper. _____

_____

READING SKILLS
Tell Fact From Opinion

Directions Read the paragraph below. Use the information in the paragraph to identify each statement as Fact or Opinion. In the blanks, write *F* if the statement is a fact and write *O* if the statement is an opinion.

James Oglethorpe

While a lawmaker in England, James Oglethorpe heard that a good friend had been sent to prison for not paying his debts. Oglethorpe hurried to the prison but arrived too late. His friend had died of smallpox. In memory of this friend, Oglethorpe decided to help debtors. One way he did this was by bringing debtors to the new colony of Georgia. Oglethorpe offered each settler a 50-acre bonus for every debtor that the settler brought along to help with the work of starting a colony. There the debtors could work for the settlers and pay back the money they owed. Oglethorpe hoped that debtors would work hard if they were given a second chance.

1 __F__ James Oglethorpe was a lawmaker in England.

2 __F__ A good friend of Oglethorpe's was in prison.

3 __F__ Oglethorpe did not arrive in time to help his friend.

4 __O__ Smallpox is the worst of all diseases.

5 __F__ Oglethorpe decided to help debtors.

6 __O__ Oglethorpe's idea to help debtors was a good one.

7 __O__ Hard work would benefit the debtors.

8 __F__ Debtors came to the Georgia Colony.

9 __O__ Oglethorpe was a good man.

Southern Plantations

Directions Read the sentences below and decide whether the information applies to slaves or indentured servants. Circle the letter under the appropriate column. Then write that letter in the appropriate blank below.

Plantation Workers	Slaves	Indentured Servants
1 Sent by the English courts to work in the colonies to pay for their crimes	S	(W)
2 Kidnapped and sold in the colonies	(E)	M
3 Came willingly to the English colonies	O	(D)
4 Sold like property at auctions	(R)	U
5 Were given their freedom after a certain length of time	H	(A)
6 Were punished by overseers if they did not work hard	(T)	C
7 Had little money to travel, so they went with others and worked off their debts	N	(T)
8 Two kinds of these workers existed: field and house	(E)	P
9 Were forbidden by law to learn how to read and write	(I)	J

Where were the earliest plantations usually built?

T	I	D	E	W	A	T	E	R
6	9	3	8	1	5	7	2	4

Name _____ Date _____

Products of the East Coast

Legend:
- Apples
- Blueberries
- Cattle
- Corn
- Dairy
- Eggs
- Hogs
- Nursery products
- Peanuts
- Poultry
- Seafood
- Soybeans
- Tobacco
- Vegetables

(continued)

Use after reading Chapter 7, Skill Lesson, pages 246–247.

Name _____ Date _____

Directions Use the map on page 68 to help you answer the questions.

1 What product is produced in every state? dairy _____

2 Where on the East Coast will you find tobacco grown? Virginia, North Carolina, _____
South Carolina _____

3 In which state are blueberries grown? Maine _____

4 Where on the East Coast will you find apples grown? Maine, New Hampshire, _____
Vermont, New York _____

5 Where are soybeans grown? Delaware, North Carolina, South Carolina, _____
Maryland, Virginia _____

6 Which two states grow exactly the same kinds of products?
Virginia and South Carolina _____

_____

7 In which state are peanuts grown? Georgia _____

8 What products are produced in South Carolina that are not produced in Maine?
tobacco, hogs, and soybeans _____

Use the map to explain what opportunities there might be for a person looking for a
job in the southern states.

Answers should show that there are many kinds of industries to choose from in

that area: tobacco, dairy, hogs, peanuts, poultry and eggs, nursery stock, and

soybeans. Students may be aware that hog farming is a huge business in North

Carolina and that nursery stock is always in demand. The dairy industry has been

growing rapidly in recent years. Dairy and hog farming and raising poultry for their

meat or eggs all are big businesses.

_____

_____

Southern Cities

Directions Fill in each blank with the correct word.

1 Some workers specialized as fishers, tailors, printers, or ____hat makers____.

2 A young person often learned a trade by becoming an ____apprentice____.

3 ____Merchants____ and ____planters____ had the most power in Charles Town society.

4 What was one reason wealthy planters lived in Charles Town during the summer months? to get away from the summer insect infestations on their plantations' wetlands

5 What did colonists find when they moved north along the Atlantic coast in search of fertile soil for plantations? What did they do with their find?

They found a lot of trees. They eventually cut down trees and built sawmills.

6 Some of Wilmington's earliest immigrants came from ____northern Scotland____

_____

7 The Georgia Colony's chief port was the coastal town of ____Savannah____.

8 What were the three products that caused Norfolk, Virginia, to grow quickly?

tobacco, naval stores, and lumber

9 In Baltimore the ____Patapsco____ River flows into the ____Chesapeake____ Bay.

10 What was the reason for Baltimore's successful shipyards?

improved ship building methods

The Southern Colonies

Directions Complete this graphic organizer by using facts you have learned from the chapter to make generalizations about the Southern Colonies.

1. Settlement of the South

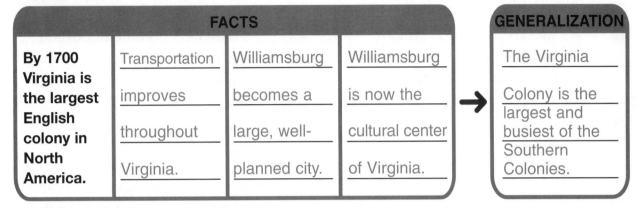

FACTS				GENERALIZATION
By 1700 Virginia is the largest English colony in North America.	Transportation improves throughout Virginia.	Williamsburg becomes a large, well-planned city.	Williamsburg is now the cultural center of Virginia.	The Virginia Colony is the largest and busiest of the Southern Colonies.

2. Southern Plantations

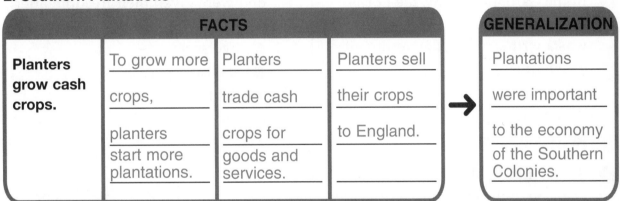

FACTS				GENERALIZATION
Planters grow cash crops.	To grow more crops, planters start more plantations.	Planters trade cash crops for goods and services.	Planters sell their crops to England.	Plantations were important to the economy of the Southern Colonies.

3. Southern Cities

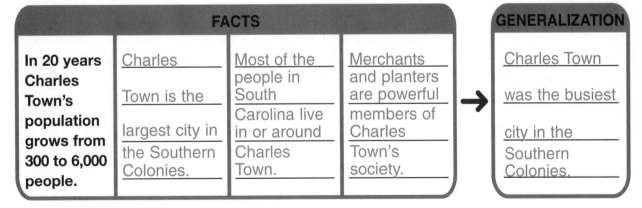

FACTS				GENERALIZATION
In 20 years Charles Town's population grows from 300 to 6,000 people.	Charles Town is the largest city in the Southern Colonies.	Most of the people in South Carolina live in or around Charles Town.	Merchants and planters are powerful members of Charles Town's society.	Charles Town was the busiest city in the Southern Colonies.

7 Test Preparation

Directions Read each question and choose the best answer. Then fill in the circle for the answer you have chosen. Be sure to fill in the circle completely.

1 The Calverts wanted to build a colony in North America to make money and provide a refuge for _____.
- Ⓐ Puritans
- ● Catholics
- Ⓒ colonists
- Ⓓ debtors

2 In the Carolina Colony, the Lords Proprietors wrote a _____, which was a written plan of government.
- Ⓕ charter
- Ⓖ action plan
- Ⓗ ratification
- ● constitution

3 By the mid-1700s _____, Virginia, was one of the most important cities in the 13 colonies.
- ● Williamsburg
- Ⓑ Savannah
- Ⓒ Baltimore
- Ⓓ Charles Town

4 _____ owners became important leaders in the 13 colonies.
- Ⓕ Ship
- Ⓖ Sawmill
- ● Plantation
- Ⓙ Land

5 Unlike _____, indentured servants were not taken against their will and were given their freedom after a certain length of time.
- Ⓐ overseers
- ● slaves
- Ⓒ debtors
- Ⓓ masters

The French and Indian War Begins

Directions Read the passage below and complete the activities that follow.

General Braddock's Defeat

General Edward Braddock was appointed the commander of all British forces in the French and Indian War. His first goal was to capture Fort Duquesne, the French stronghold. In April 1755 he led more than 1,800 British and colonial troops westward across the mountains. The trip was long and difficult for the soldiers as they moved the large wagons and artillery across the rough trails.

Meanwhile, the French had learned of the British advance and were waiting. About 8 miles from Fort Duquesne, the French and their Native American allies attacked the British from behind trees and boulders. The British were trained to fight in open fields and had never fought an enemy this way. After the battle, almost two-thirds of the British troops were dead or wounded, including General Braddock. He died four days later.

Directions For numbers 1–5, write *T* next to the statements that are true and *F* next to the statements that are false.

1. __F__ General Braddock was the commander of all British forces in the Revolutionary War.

2. __T__ Braddock's army had a difficult journey to Fort Duquesne.

3. __T__ The French were aware that Braddock's army was approaching.

4. __F__ The British were trained to fight in wooded areas.

5. __F__ General Braddock died immediately after being wounded on the battlefield.

Directions For numbers 6–10, write *F* if the statement is a fact or *O* if the statement is an opinion.

6. __O__ The French were excellent fighters.

7. __F__ The Native Americans were allies of the French.

8. __O__ General Braddock was nervous about the journey to Fort Duquesne.

9. __F__ Moving large artillery was difficult.

10. __F__ Braddock's army consisted of British and colonial troops.

Name _____ Date _____

Britain Wins North America

Directions Number the sentences below in the order in which each event occurred.

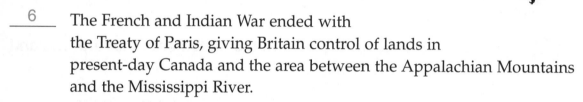

___5___ To make up for Spain's losses in the war, France gave Spain most of Louisiana and part of what is now Florida.

___7___ Native Americans did not welcome the British colonists who wanted to settle in the Ohio Valley after the Treaty of Paris was signed.

___1___ The British captured three forts: Fort Duquesne, Louisbourg, and Frontenac.

___6___ The French and Indian War ended with the Treaty of Paris, giving Britain control of lands in present-day Canada and the area between the Appalachian Mountains and the Mississippi River.

___9___ Many Native American fighters signed peace treaties with the British.

___3___ French forces were defeated by General James Wolfe's British troops on the Plains of Abraham, near Quebec.

___4___ The French gave up after the British captured Montreal.

___2___ The British captured forts at Crown Point, Niagara, and Ticonderoga.

___8___ Chief Pontiac united with other Native American tribes and attacked British forts.

___10___ King George III issued the Proclamation of 1763, which prevented British colonists from buying, hunting on, or exploring land west of the Appalachian Mountains.

(continued)

Use after reading Chapter 8, Lesson 2, pages 273–277.

Name _____ Date _____

1 Why did King George III order the Proclamation of 1763?

King George believed that stopping the westward movement of British colonists

was the only way to prevent more wars between the colonists and Native

Americans.

2 What effects did the proclamation have on the life of the British colonists?

The land west of the Appalachians was off-limits to the colonists. They could no

longer buy, hunt on, or explore it; any colonist already living there was ordered

to leave.

3 How did the American colonists feel about the proclamation? Why did they feel

this way? It angered the colonists because they felt the proclamation took away

their right as British citizens to travel where they wanted.

4 According to the British colonists, how did the Proclamation of 1763 conflict with

the English Bill of Rights? The English Bill of Rights gave the colonists the same

rights as all British citizens. The colonists believed the proclamation took away

these rights.

5 Did the proclamation stop colonists from settling west of the Appalachians?

Explain. No. Even though colonists were not supposed to use the land, colonial

pioneers continued to push westward into the frontier.

Name _____ Date _____

MAP AND GLOBE SKILLS
Compare Historical Maps

Directions Use the maps to answer the questions on both pages.

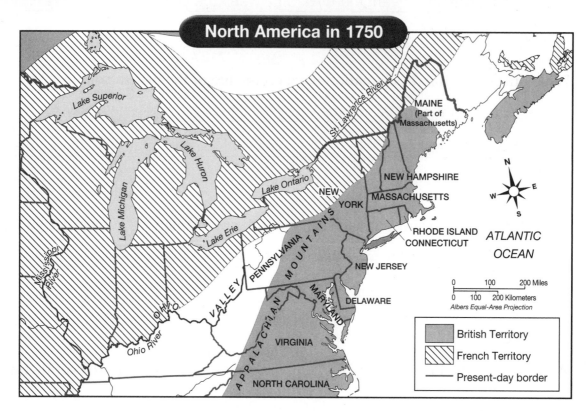

North America in 1750

MAINE (Part of Massachusetts)
NEW HAMPSHIRE
MASSACHUSETTS
NEW YORK
RHODE ISLAND
CONNECTICUT
NEW JERSEY
DELAWARE
PENNSYLVANIA
MARYLAND
VIRGINIA
NORTH CAROLINA

Lake Superior
Lake Huron
Lake Michigan
Lake Ontario
Lake Erie
St. Lawrence River
Mississippi River
Ohio River
VALLEY
APPALACHIAN MOUNTAINS
OHIO

ATLANTIC OCEAN

0   100   200 Miles
0   100   200 Kilometers
Albers Equal-Area Projection

British Territory
French Territory
Present-day border

1 What pattern is used to show land originally claimed by the British and then given to the Native Americans? hatch lines _____

2 According to the map, was any land claimed by the French in North America in 1763? no _____

3 What land areas once claimed by the French were later claimed by the British?
the land near the Mississippi River

4 Before the French and Indian War, who occupied the territory along the St. Lawrence River? the French _____

5 Before 1763, who claimed most of the land north of the Ohio River?
the French

(continued)

Use after reading Chapter 8, Skill Lesson, pages 278–279.

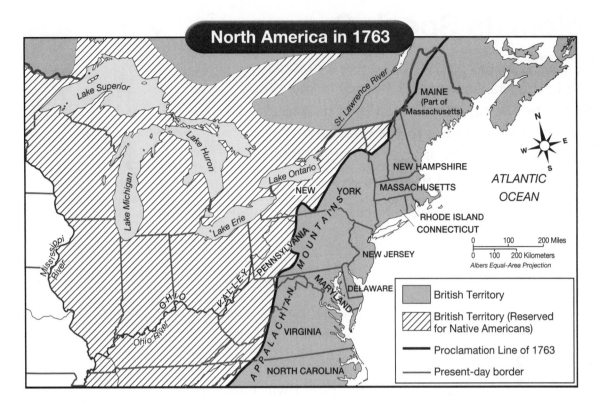

North America in 1763

6 Who claimed the region of present-day Kentucky after the French and
Indian War? the British

7 When did the British claim the regions bordering the Atlantic Ocean, such as
Massachusetts, Connecticut, and Rhode Island? both before and after the
French and Indian War

8 Imagine that you are an explorer living in 1750. Write a description of the
following journey: You start in what is now Maine and travel to the New York
Colony, then to the region now known as Michigan, and then to the Ohio Valley
region. How did you travel? Who claimed the land in which you traveled?
What direction did you take? What kind of people did you encounter?

Student answers will vary. Possible answer: I would travel by land or by boat

to New York. Then journey across New York to the Great Lakes and into Michigan

and the Ohio Valley. My journey began in British territory then moved into French

territory. I encountered other colonists, Native Americans, and some French and

British troops.

Colonists Speak Out

Directions Imagine that you are a colonist living in the Massachusetts Colony in the 1760s and you are being interviewed by a newspaper reporter. Write answers to the interview questions. Be sure to answer the questions from a colonist's point of view.

1 Many people like you are angry about the Sugar Act. What is the Sugar Act, and why has it angered you? Possible answer: The Sugar Act adds taxes on sugar and other goods coming to the colonies from other places. This means we have to pay more for goods. The act angers me and my fellow colonists because we believe our rights as British citizens have been violated.

2 Soon after the Sugar Act, the Stamp Act was enacted. How is the Stamp Act similar to the Sugar Act? Possible answer: Both acts force us to pay taxes. Again, we feel our rights as British citizens have been violated.

3 What can you do to show you are against taxation without representation? Possible answer: Many of us are refusing to buy goods that have been stamped. We are also boycotting many British goods. Some women in our town are making their own cloth so that we do not have to buy cloth from Britain.

4 Why are there so many British soldiers in Massachusetts and the other colonies? How do you feel about the soldiers being here? Possible answer: Parliament is trying to show its authority over us by sending many soldiers. Having these soldiers here angers not only me but also my fellow colonists.

CITIZENSHIP SKILLS
Determine Point of View

Directions Read each statement and then decide whose point of view the statement represents. Write either "Colonist" or "British leader" in the blank space before the sentence. In the second blank space, explain why each person might hold this point of view.

1 _____British leader_____ We need money to help pay the cost of the French and Indian War.

The British Parliament discussed this in its 1764 budget before it passed new

laws that taxed the colonists.

2 _____Colonist_____ The Sugar Act is unjust. We had no representation when this law was decided.

The colonists did not have a voice in Parliament and believed their rights had

been violated.

3 _____British leader_____ Patrick Henry has committed treason. He is working against his government.

British leaders in the colonies thought Patrick Henry was against the government

because he did not agree with Parliament's new laws.

4 _____Colonist_____ We need to work together instead of acting separately. We should talk with other colonial leaders to discuss what to do about the Stamp Act.

Colonial leaders thought it was better for the colonies to work together, so they

held a meeting. Nine colonies sent representatives to this meeting to talk about

the new taxes.

5 _____Colonist_____ We do not want "lobsters" and "redcoats" in our cities!

Colonists were angry at the great numbers of British soldiers being sent to the

13 colonies.

The Road to War

Directions Use the Word Bank
to complete each sentence.

Lexington	quarter
Samuel Adams	monopoly
Minutemen	Sons of Liberty
petition	Paul Revere
Intolerable Acts	blockade

1. Parliament wanted to give the East India Company a _____monopoly_____ on tea.

2. _____Samuel Adams_____ believed in the use of violence only when all else failed.

3. A group of men called the _____Sons of Liberty_____ boarded ships and dumped tea into the harbor.

4. To keep ships from entering or leaving Boston Harbor, Parliament ordered

   a _____blockade_____.

5. Colonists were punished by having to _____quarter_____ British soldiers.

6. The colonists called Parliament's new laws the _____Intolerable Acts_____.

7. The First Continental Congress sent Parliament a _____petition_____, which stated that colonists had a right to "life, liberty, and property."

8. Colonists in Massachusetts organized a militia made up of

   _____Minutemen_____.

9. When he learned the British were coming, _____Paul Revere_____ rode to Lexington to warn fellow colonists.

10. The fighting at _____Lexington_____ and Concord marked the beginning of the Revolutionary War.

The Second Continental Congress

Directions Imagine that you are a member of the Second Continental Congress. Write a letter to King George III explaining why you believe the colonies in North America should be allowed to peacefully separate from Britain.

Think about these questions as you write your letter:

What was John Dickinson's point of view on war?

How many people died in the battle at Breed's Hill?

How might a petition help?

Who, other than the British and colonists, might be affected by war?

Students' letters may indicate that a peaceful separation is better because it avoids many deaths. They may also argue that too many people have died already. They may explain that a petition is a peaceful approach to solving a problem. They may indicate that Native Americans will be caught up in the war.

Events Unite the Colonies

Directions Complete this graphic organizer to show that you understand the causes and effects of some of the key events that helped unite the colonies.

 Cause → **Effect**

Cause	Effect
The British Parliament needs extra money to pay for the French and Indian War.	The British Parliament taxes the colonists.
Colonists are angry about the British government's tax on tea.	The Boston Tea Party takes place in Boston Harbor in December 1773.
The British Parliament passes the Intolerable Acts to punish the colonists.	The First Continental Congress is held.
The Minutemen and the British fight at Lexington and Concord.	The Second Continental Congress is held in Philadelphia in May 1775.
The Battle of Bunker Hill takes place near Boston on June 17, 1775.	Britain's King George III issues a proclamation of rebellion.

Name _____   Date _____

8 Test Preparation

Directions Read each question and choose the best answer. Then fill in the circle for the answer you have chosen. Be sure to fill in the circle completely.

1 The French and Indian War began because both France and Britain believed they owned the area known as—
- Ⓐ Pennsylvania.
- Ⓑ the Appalachians.
- Ⓒ the Ohio Valley.
- Ⓓ New France.

2 Chief Pontiac's rebellion began because he—
- Ⓕ believed he owned the Ohio Valley region.
- Ⓖ wanted to stop the loss of Indian hunting lands.
- Ⓗ had formed an alliance with France.
- Ⓙ wanted to rule British forts.

3 Why were colonists angered by the tax laws passed by the British Parliament?
- Ⓐ They believed they should have a voice in deciding such laws.
- Ⓑ They were too poor to pay the taxes.
- Ⓒ They thought the taxes were unfair.
- Ⓓ They believed they shouldn't have to pay any taxes.

4 Which of the following was an Intolerable Act?
- Ⓕ preventing the Massachusetts legislature from making laws
- Ⓖ banning any town meetings not authorized by the governor
- Ⓗ forcing colonists to quarter British soldiers
- Ⓙ all of the above

5 The first united colonial army was called—
- Ⓐ the Continental Army.
- Ⓑ the Hessian Army.
- Ⓒ the Mercenary Army.
- Ⓓ the Loyalist Army.

Independence Is Declared

Directions Use words and phrases from the Word Bank to complete each sentence below.

public opinion	Preamble	resolution
allegiance	independence	grievances

1 The point of view held by most people is called _____public opinion_____.

2 The colonists wanted _____independence_____, the freedom to govern themselves.

3 Another word for loyalty is _____allegiance_____.

4 Richard Henry Lee wrote a formal statement, known as a

_____resolution_____, describing the feelings of the colonists.

5 The first part of the Declaration of Independence is called the

_____Preamble_____.

6 The complaints, or _____grievances_____, against the British king and Parliament were part of the Declaration of Independence.

(continued)

Use after reading Chapter 9, Lesson 1, pages 302–307.

Name _____ Date _____

Directions Match each person with the correct description. Write the letter of the correct person on the blank provided. Some letters may be used more than once.

Description   **Name**

7 __D__ first to sign the Declaration   **A.** John Dickinson
              of Independence
                                                       B. John Adams
8 __F__ wrote the Declaration
              of Independence   **C.** John Nixon

9 __B__ wrote a letter to his wife Abigail   **D.** John Hancock
              describing the first public reading
              of the Declaration of Independence   **E.** Thomas Paine

10 __E__ published *Common Sense* in   **F.** Thomas Jefferson
              January, 1776

11 __A__ helped write the Articles of
              the Confederation

12 __C__ read the Declaration of
              Independence to the
              Second Continental Congress

13 __F__ wrote *A Summary View of the
              Rights of British America*

14 __E__ called for a revolution before the
              Declaration of Independence was written

Americans and the Revolution

Directions Read the passage below. When you have finished, write a paragraph trying to persuade someone to choose a different position in the Revolutionary War. For example, you may try to persuade a Loyalist to become a Patriot.

As the Revolutionary War began, most colonists held one of four opinions. Those who supported the British king and Parliament were called **Loyalists.** They wanted to work out the differences between the colonies and Britain. Those people who were **Patriots** wanted to break from Britain and form a new country. They believed they could establish a better government if they were independent.

Some people wanted to wait and see what would happen. They did not want to take either side. They were **neutral** about the matter of independence and willing to accept whatever happened. Some people, such as Quakers, were opposed to war for any reason. They were known as **pacifists,** or people who believe in settling disagreements peacefully.

Use after reading Chapter 9, Lesson 2, pages 308–312.

Name _____ Date _____

CITIZENSHIP SKILLS
Make a Decision

Directions The Revolutionary War has begun. How will you respond? Explain your decision, based on the questions below.

Steps in Making a Decision

1 Know that you have to make a decision.

You have the choice of fighting for the British or for the colonists.

2 Gather information.

What do you need to know before deciding? Where might you find the information you need?

Students should state that they need to know what each side is fighting for.

Students should state that they could find this information by talking to people.

3 Identify your choices.

There are at least two choices, as given above. Are there other choices you could make?

Students' answers should include remaining neutral or taking a pacifist position.

4 Predict consequences, and weigh those consequences.

List each of the choices with its consequences. If a consequence seems very important to you, put a star next to it.

Students' answers will vary, but should indicate which consequence seems most

important to them.

5 Make a choice, and take action.

What will you decide?

Students' answers will vary but should give reasons that support their decisions.

Fighting the Revolutionary War

Directions Follow the instructions below. Write your answers on the map.

1 Draw a star next to the battle known as the turning point of the war. Saratoga

2 Circle the place where Ethan Allen and the Green Mountain boys were victorious. Fort Ticonderoga

3 Draw a snowflake next to the place where Washington's troops spent the winter of 1777. Valley Forge

4 Draw a pitcher at the battle where Mary Ludwig Hays McCauley brought water to the soldiers. Monmouth

5 Draw a boat where Washington surprised Hessian mercenaries on Christmas Day, 1776. Trenton

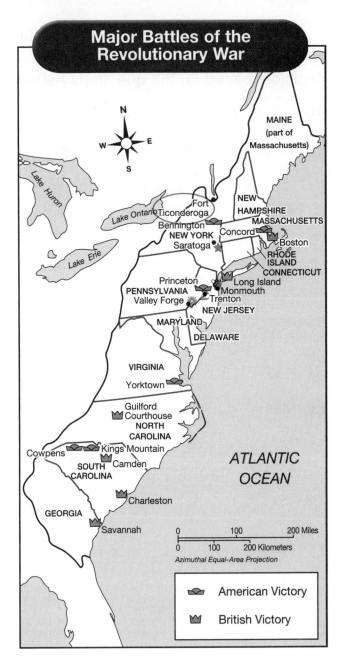

Major Battles of the Revolutionary War

MAINE (part of Massachusetts)

Lake Huron

Lake Ontario

Lake Erie

Fort Ticonderoga

Bennington
NEW YORK
Saratoga

NEW HAMPSHIRE
MASSACHUSETTS
Concord
Boston
RHODE ISLAND
CONNECTICUT

Princeton
PENNSYLVANIA
Valley Forge
Trenton

Long Island
Monmouth

NEW JERSEY

MARYLAND

DELAWARE

VIRGINIA

Yorktown

Guilford
Courthouse
NORTH
CAROLINA

Cowpens
SOUTH
CAROLINA

Kings Mountain
Camden

Charleston

GEORGIA

Savannah

ATLANTIC OCEAN

0   100   200 Miles
0   100   200 Kilometers
Azimuthal Equal-Area Projection

American Victory

British Victory

Use after reading Chapter 9, Lesson 3, pages 314–319.

Independence Is Won

Directions Complete the time line using the choices listed below. Write the number of the event next to the correct marker on the time line.

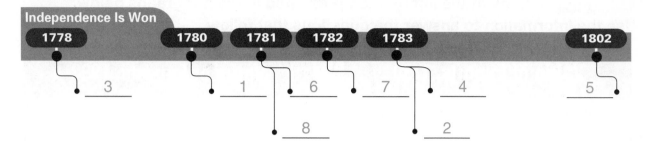

Independence Is Won

| 1778 | 1780 | 1781 | 1782 | 1783 | 1802 |

3   1   6   7   4   5

8   2

1 British capture Charleston, South Carolina 1780

2 George Washington returns to Virginia 1783

3 British capture Savannah, Georgia 1778

4 Britain and the United States sign the Treaty of Paris 1783

5 The United States Military Academy is founded at West Point 1802

6 British surrender at Yorktown 1781

7 Britain and the United States send representatives to Paris 1782

8 The Continental Army wins the Battle of Cowpens 1781

Name _____ Date _____

CHART AND GRAPH SKILLS

Compare Graphs

Directions Look at the information presented in the bar graphs below. Use the information to answer the questions that follow.

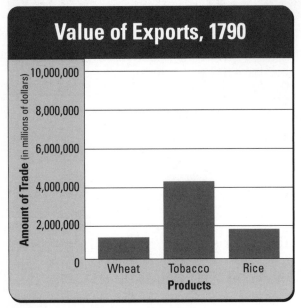

Source: *A History of Commerce* by Clive Day Longmans, Green and Co.

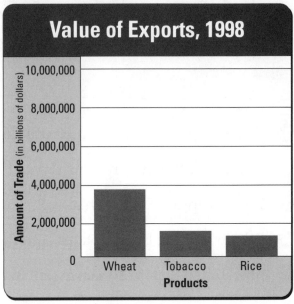

Source: Statistical Abstract of the United States

1 Compare the two graphs. How has the relative importance of each item's dollar value changed? Answers may vary. Students may point out that wheat was once the smallest export but now is the most important in value. Others may point out that tobacco is no longer the country's leading agricultural export.

2 About how much more valuable were tobacco exports compared to wheat exports in 1790? about 2.7 million dollars

3 About how much more valuable were wheat exports compared to tobacco exports in 1998? about 2.4 billion dollars

(continued)

Use after reading Chapter 9, Skill Lesson, pages 330–331.

Name _____   Date _____

Directions Look at the information presented in the line graphs below. Use the graphs to answer the questions that follow.

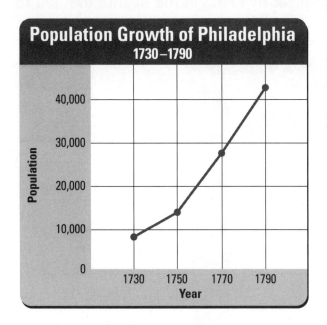

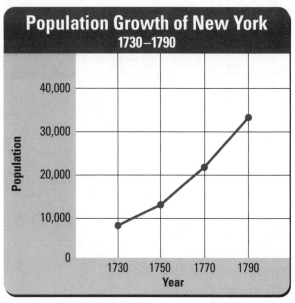

4 Which city grew faster from 1730 to 1790? Philadelphia _____

5 In what years were the two cities equal or nearly equal in population?

1730 and 1750 _____

6 In 1770, about how many more people lived in Philadelphia than in New York?

about 7,000 _____

7 By how many times did the population of Philadelphia grow over the 60 years

the graph covers? The population grew about five times its original size. _____

8 What was the growth in New York during the same time period?

The population grew to about four times its original size. _____

Independence Is Declared

Directions Complete this graphic organizer by filling in the events that led to the colonies declaring independence.

FIRST	NEXT	LAST
Colonists in North America want independence for the 13 British Colonies	Congress approves and signs the Declaration of Independence	The 13 American Colonies declare their independence from the British

Name _____ Date _____

9 Test Preparation

Directions Read each question and choose the best answer. Then fill in the circle for the answer you have chosen. Be sure to fill in the circle completely.

1 Which of the following was **not** a reason American colonists wanted to break with Britain in 1776?

- Ⓐ taxes
- Ⓑ no representation
- Ⓒ religious freedom
- Ⓓ war had already begun

2 Who was the author of the Declaration of Independence?

- Ⓕ Thomas Paine
- Ⓖ John Adams
- Ⓗ Richard Henry Lee
- Ⓙ Thomas Jefferson

3 People who remained neutral in the war—

- Ⓐ sided with the colonists.
- Ⓑ took neither side.
- Ⓒ did not believe war was right.
- Ⓓ were loyal to Britain.

4 Which of the following countries did **not** send help to the colonies?

- Ⓕ Scotland
- Ⓖ France
- Ⓗ Poland
- Ⓙ Spain

5 General Cornwallis surrendered at the Battle of—

- Ⓐ Fort Ticonderoga.
- Ⓑ Saratoga.
- Ⓒ Charlestown.
- Ⓓ Yorktown.

Name _____ Date _____

The Confederation Period

Directions Each statement below is false. For each sentence, cross out the wrong word. Then, in the blank at the end of the sentence, write the word that would make the sentence true.

1 After the war with Britain ended, Congress printed too much money, causing terrible ~~rebellion~~. inflation _____

2 A form of government in which people elect representatives to govern the country is called a ~~dictatorship~~. republic _____

3 Decision making required representation from at least ~~five~~ states.

nine _____

4 Shays's Rebellion started over ~~army policy~~. taxes _____

5 Shays's Rebellion took place in ~~Virginia~~. Massachusetts _____

6 An arsenal is a place to store ~~food~~. weapons _____

7 A territory is land that belongs to the ~~state~~ government but is not represented in Congress. national _____

8 Congress passed an ~~arsenal~~, or set of laws, to measure the western lands.

ordinance _____

9 The newly settled lands were called the ~~Southeast~~ Territory.

Northwest _____

10 Townships were ~~8~~ miles on each side. 6 _____

11 The new lands were to offer ~~private~~ schools to everyone.

public _____

The Constitutional Convention

Directions Read the following list of issues debated at the Constitutional Convention. Match the resolution of each one with the correct issue. Write the letter of the correct resolution on the blank provided.

1 __B__ the relationship between the states and national government

2 __C__ representation of each state in Congress

3 __A__ the issue of enslaved African Americans

A. the Three-Fifths Compromise

B. a federal system of shared powers

C. a system of two houses of Congress

Directions Read each sentence below, and fill in the blank with the correct term. Use the words from the Word Bank.

| George Read | George Washington | Roger Sherman |
| Rhode Island | Benjamin Franklin | |

4 All the states except __Rhode Island__ sent delegates to Philadelphia.

5 The oldest member of the convention was __Benjamin Franklin__.

6 The delegates elected __George Washington__ president of the convention.

7 __George Read__ believed that states should be done away with altogether.

8 The Connecticut Compromise was created by __Roger Sherman__.

Name _____ Date _____

The Three Branches of Government

Directions Read the list below of positions in the government. In the space provided, name the correct branch of government for each one. Then write a brief description of the qualifications and duties of the person holding that job.

1 President Executive; serves for 4 years,

must be at least 35 years old, must have

been born in the United States or have

parents who were born in the United States.

A President has veto power, is commander in chief of the armed forces, and

represents the country to other nations.

_____

_____

2 Supreme Court Justice Judicial; appointed by the President for life, subject to

Senate approval; hears cases dealing with the Constitution, national law,

or treaties.

_____

_____

_____

3 Representative Legislative; serves for 2 years, must be at least 25 years old,

must have been a citizen for 7 years, must live in the state he or she represents.

Representatives can make laws, declare war, coin money, and originate

tax bills.

_____

_____

_____

Use after reading Chapter 10, Lesson 3, pages 358–363.

Name _____ Date _____

CHART AND GRAPH SKILLS
Read a Flow Chart

Directions Fill in the flow chart to show the jobs in each of the three branches of government. In the second row, describe the main task of each branch. Some examples have been filled in for you.

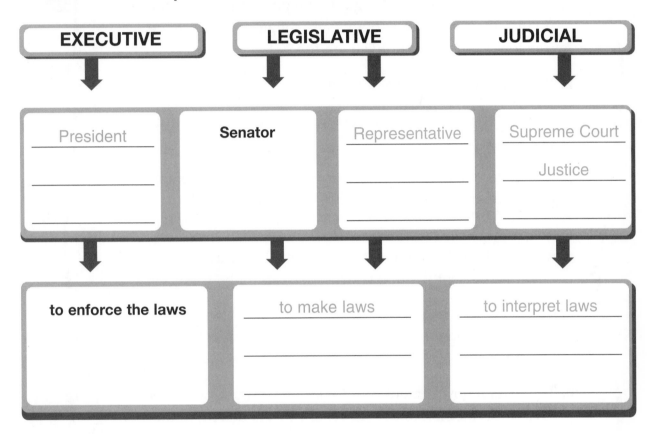

EXECUTIVE	LEGISLATIVE	JUDICIAL
President	Senator Representative	Supreme Court Justice
to enforce the laws	to make laws	to interpret laws

Name _____ Date _____

Approval and the Bill of Rights

Directions Read the freedoms guaranteed by the Bill of Rights. Then read each statement that follows. If the statement is a fact, write *F* in the blank. If the statement is an opinion, write *O* in the blank.

1. People may follow any religion. The government cannot financially support or promote any religion. People have freedom to speak, to publish, and to hold meetings.

2. People may keep and bear weapons.

3. People do not have to board soldiers in their homes during peacetime.

4. The government cannot search people's homes or remove their property without the permission of a judge.

5–8. People have the right to a fair trial by a jury. Defendants do not have to testify against themselves. They may have a lawyer represent them in court. They cannot be tried twice for the same crime.

9. People have other rights not specifically listed in the Constitution.

10. The federal government can do only what the Constitution gives it permission to do. All other powers belong to the states and to the people.

1 __O__ It is not fair to have soldiers sleeping in your home at any time.

2 __F__ People can hold public meetings to talk about their government.

3 __O__ Newspapers should print only good news.

4 __O__ The federal government has gotten too powerful.

5 __F__ A person cannot be tried twice for the same crime.

6 __O__ The individual states do not have enough power.

7 __F__ People do not have to testify against themselves in court.

Name _____ Date _____

CITIZENSHIP SKILLS
Act as a Responsible Citizen

Directions Citizens have responsibilities as well as rights and privileges.
Read each statement below the picture. Then suggest how a responsible
citizen might handle the situation.

1 You notice that people are being careless about litter in your neighborhood.

Answers will vary but may suggest picking up litter, organizing a group to

monitor litter, or petitioning for more trash containers to be placed in public areas.

2 Several dogs in your neighborhood are not on leashes.

Answers will vary but may suggest creating or enforcing leash laws.

3 Skateboarders in your neighborhood are practicing on sidewalks and in the street.

Answers will vary but may suggest trying to persuade local officials to designate

a skateboard park area.

4 A local election is coming up. Answers will vary but should indicate that a

responsible citizen would vote.

5 A new law is coming up for discussion before being voted on. Some people

disagree with the law. Answers will vary but may suggest writing a letter to the

editor of a local newspaper or attending local political meetings to express

opinions.

The New Government Begins

Directions The two major political parties of the late eighteenth century differed in several ways. Fill out the chart below to show how they were different. One example has been given.

FEDERALIST	REPUBLICAN
Believed in a strong central government	Believed that the powers of the national government should be limited to those stated in the Constitution
Answers may include the following:	Answers may include the following:
Believed government should	Believed the economy should
encourage manufacturing; Believed	depend on agriculture; Believed the
the United States should have close	United States should have close
ties with Britain; Wanted a federal	ties with France; Wanted little
bank to issue paper money; Were	government; Were followers
followers of Hamilton	of Jefferson

Use after reading Chapter 10, Lesson 5, pages 374–379.

A New Form of Government

Directions Complete this graphic organizer by summarizing the facts about the writing and ratification of the United States Constitution.

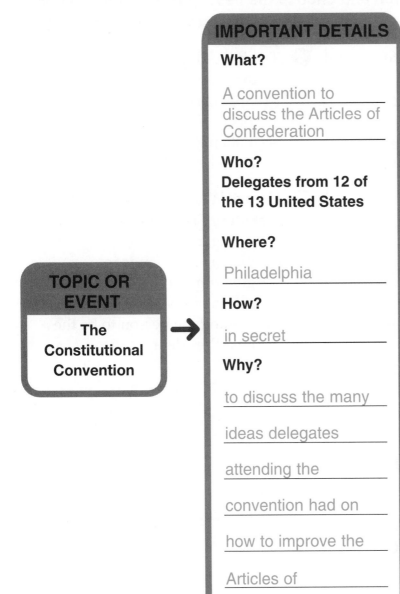

TOPIC OR EVENT

The Constitutional Convention

IMPORTANT DETAILS

What?
A convention to discuss the Articles of Confederation

Who?
Delegates from 12 of the 13 United States

Where?
Philadelphia

How?
in secret

Why?
to discuss the many ideas delegates attending the convention had on how to improve the Articles of Confederation

SUMMARY

Delegates to the Philadelphia Convention met to discuss ways to improve upon the Articles of Confederation. Instead, the Convention delegates decided to do away with the Articles and create a new form of government.

Name _____ Date _____

10 Test Preparation

Directions Read each question and choose the best answer. Then fill in the circle for the answer you have chosen. Be sure to fill in the circle completely.

1 _____ was one good reason for changing the weak national government set up by the Articles of Confederation.
- Ⓐ The Northwest Ordinance
- Ⓑ The way Congress moved around
- ⒸShays's Rebellion
- Ⓓ The idea of James Madison

2 The Great Compromise established—
- Ⓕ how enslaved African Americans would be counted.
- Ⓖ who had the right to tax.
- Ⓗ the balance between state and federal government.
- Ⓙhow states would be represented in Congress.

3 A President who does not perform the duties of the office can be—
- Ⓐimpeached by Congress.
- Ⓑ forced to leave town.
- Ⓒ tried before the Supreme Court.
- Ⓓ sent to a foreign country.

4 The Bill of Rights was influenced by the—
- Ⓕ Spanish constitution.
- ⒼBritish Magna Carta.
- Ⓗ Italian Bill of Rights.
- Ⓙ French political practice.

5 George Washington set an example for future Presidents by—
- Ⓐ riding a white horse.
- Ⓑ placing his friends in government positions.
- Ⓒserving only two elected terms.
- Ⓓ naming the person to be the next President.

Use after reading Chapter 10, pages 344–379.

The Louisiana Purchase

Directions Read each numbered item below. Fill in each blank with the name of the person or persons connected to the description. Use names from the Word Bank. You may use a name more than once.

Sacagawea	Thomas Jefferson	Meriwether Lewis	Zebulon Pike
York	William Clark	Napoleon Bonaparte	

1 hoped to revive French power in North America

Napoleon Bonaparte

2 wanted the United States to have a port on the lower Mississippi River

Thomas Jefferson

3 needed money to fight a war Napoleon Bonaparte

4 leaders of the Corps of Discovery Meriwether Lewis and William Clark

5 African American who helped the Corps of Discovery by hunting and fishing

York

6 helped the Corps of Discovery by guiding them through the land of the

Shoshones Sacagawea

7 explored the southwestern portion of the Louisiana Purchase

Zebulon Pike

The War of 1812

Directions Look at the time line below. Match the events with the correct date on the time line. Place the letter of the correct event in the blank provided.

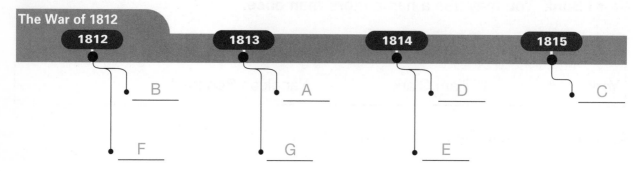

A. Battle of Lake Erie

B. United States declares war against Britain

C. Battle of New Orleans

D. British burn Washington, D.C.

E. Francis Scott Key writes "The Defense of Fort McHenry"

F. The warship *Constitution* defeats the British ship *Guerriére*.

G. Battle of the Thames

(continued)

Name _____   Date _____

Directions **Answer the questions below.**

1. Give two reasons that the United States declared war on Britain.

   The British in Canada supplied Native

   Americans with guns and impressed

   United States sailors.

2. What United States senator believed that the United States should "take the whole

   continent"? Henry Clay

3. What was the nickname of the warship *Constitution*? Old Ironsides

4. What Shawnee Indian leader was killed at the Battle of the Thames?

   Tecumseh

5. What action did Dolley Madison take before leaving the White House?

   She saved important government papers and a portrait of George Washington.

6. What did Francis Scott Key do after seeing the battle at Fort McHenry?

   He wrote the poem that later became known as "The Star-Spangled Banner."

7. What years came to be known as the Era of Good Feelings?

   1817–1825

8. Why was the Battle of New Orleans unnecessary? A peace treaty between the

   British and the Americans had been signed two weeks before, on

   December 24, 1814.

The Age of Jackson

Directions Read the paragraph below. Fill in the graphic organizer to show why the United States Supreme Court said the Cherokees could keep their land. Then answer the questions that follow.

United States Supreme Court Chief Justice John Marshall wrote the opinion of the Court in the case of *Worcester* v. *Georgia*. Marshall referred to Britain's past treaties with the Cherokee. He said the Cherokee had honored the treaties. That proved that the Cherokee were a nation able to govern themselves. He also argued that the laws of Georgia had no power over the Cherokee nation people because they were a "distinct community." Finally, Marshall said that the Native Americans had previous possession of the land. It was theirs. Unfortunately, President Andrew Jackson refused to accept the ruling. He said, "John Marshall has made his decision; now let him enforce it." Jackson then ordered federal troops to remove the Native Americans and take the land.

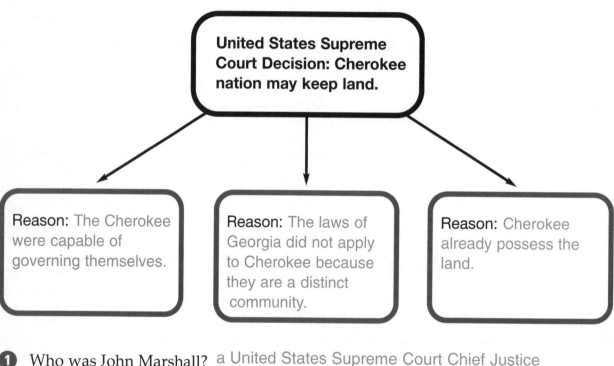

United States Supreme Court Decision: Cherokee nation may keep land.

Reason: The Cherokee were capable of governing themselves.

Reason: The laws of Georgia did not apply to Cherokee because they are a distinct community.

Reason: Cherokee already possess the land.

1 Who was John Marshall? a United States Supreme Court Chief Justice

2 What did President Andrew Jackson say about Marshall's decision?

"John Marshall has made his decision; now let him enforce it."

_____

3 What did Jackson then do? President Jackson ordered federal troops to remove

the Native Americans and take their land.

From Ocean to Ocean

Directions Fill in the blanks in the paragraph below, using terms from the Word Bank.

Mormons	gold rush	dictator	forty-niners
Oregon	Cession	manifest destiny	

In the early 1800s many people began to believe that the United States should stretch from the Atlantic Ocean to the Pacific Ocean. This idea was known as _____manifest destiny_____. In time, this goal seemed possible. In 1834 when General Santa Anna took over the Mexican government and made himself _____dictator_____, Texas settlers were alarmed. After battles at the Alamo and San Jacinto, the settlers defeated Santa Anna and Texas became an independent republic. Several years later, Mexico and the United States again clashed over the Texas border. Mexico agreed to give up its claims in what was called the Mexican _____Cession_____. In addition, some people went west in search of religious freedom. The _____Mormons_____ settled in Utah after being driven from Illinois. Marcus and Narcissa Whitman went to the _____Oregon_____ Territory to set up missions. Finally, when gold was discovered in California, a _____gold rush_____ began. Those who went called themselves _____forty-niners_____ because many settlers moved there in 1849.

Name _____ Date _____

MAP AND GLOBE SKILLS

Identifying Changing Borders

Directions Use the map below to answer the questions that follow.

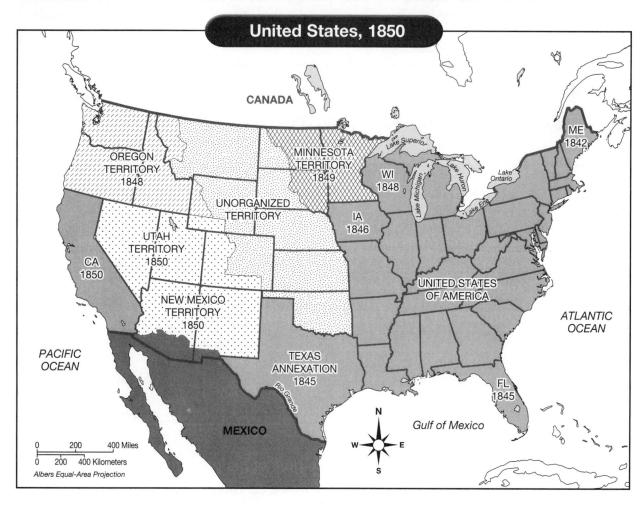

United States, 1850

CANADA

ME 1842

OREGON TERRITORY 1848

MINNESOTA TERRITORY 1849

Lake Superior

WI 1848

Lake Michigan

Lake Huron

Lake Ontario

Lake Erie

UNORGANIZED TERRITORY

IA 1846

UTAH TERRITORY 1850

CA 1850

NEW MEXICO TERRITORY 1850

UNITED STATES OF AMERICA

ATLANTIC OCEAN

PACIFIC OCEAN

TEXAS ANNEXATION 1845

Rio Grande

FL 1845

MEXICO

N

Gulf of Mexico

W   E

S

0   200   400 Miles
0   200   400 Kilometers
Albers Equal-Area Projection

1 In what year did the United States gain control of the Utah Territory? _1850_

2 What state was the farthest west in 1850? California

3 What river eventually became the border between Mexico and the United States?

Rio Grande

4 By 1850 had the idea of manifest destiny been achieved? Explain.

Yes; Possible answer: By 1850 the United States had control of the Oregon

Territory and had gained California as a state. The United States now stretched

from the Atlantic to the Pacific Ocean.

An Industrial Revolution

Directions **Tell how each invention listed below played a part in the Industrial Revolution. Write your answers on the blanks provided.** Students' answers will vary; possible answers are given.

1 The steam engine The steam engine was used in both boats and trains. It reduced the time and cost of travel and shipping.

2 Cotton mills The machines to spin thread and weave cloth cut the time needed to make fabric. Mills were the first examples of large-scale manufacturing in the United States. People began working in factories instead of at home.

3 Interchangeable parts This made mass production possible. The supply of manufactured goods increased.

4 Cotton gin The cotton gin removed seeds from cotton faster than people could. This allowed cotton to be cleaned and prepared for market in less time.

5 Mechanical reaper The reaper allowed farmers to harvest as much wheat in one day as they could in two weeks using hand tools.

Use after reading Chapter 11, Lesson 5, pages 412–419.

America and the Industrial Revolution

Directions Complete this graphic organizer by drawing conclusions about the Industrial Revolution.

WHAT YOU KNOW	NEW FACTS	CONCLUSION
Student answers will vary. Sample answer: At the time, most Americans had never been anywhere outside of the United States.	Life was often difficult for Americans, especially those who chose to settle in unexplored lands.	The Industrial Revolution made the lives of most Americans much easier, improving the ways many people lived, traveled, and worked.
Student answers will vary. Sample answer: At one time, Americans did most farming work by hand.	With new inventions like the reaper, wheat that once took two weeks to cut could now be cut in one day.	
Student answers will vary. Sample answer: Traveling in the United States was once very difficult and took a great deal of time.	By the mid-1800s more than 88 thousand miles of road and 9 thousand miles of rail had been built in the United States.	

Use after reading Chapter 11, pages 383–419.

Name _____   Date _____

11 Test Preparation

Directions Read each question and choose the best answer. Then fill in the circle for the answer you have chosen. Be sure to fill in the circle completely.

1 Napoleon was willing to sell Louisiana because—

ⓐ he knew he was too far away to control it.

ⓑ he had no use for the land.

Ⓒ he needed money to fight a war.

ⓓ he was persuaded by Jefferson's representatives.

2 The years from 1817 to 1825 are called—

ⓕ the Age of Jackson.

ⓖ manifest destiny.

ⓗ the Monroe Doctrine.

Ⓙ the Era of Good Feelings.

3 All of the following are reasons for Andrew Jackson's election *except* that—

ⓐ he was a war hero.

Ⓑ he had lots of money.

ⓒ for the first time all white men could vote.

ⓓ he was considered a common man.

4 During the 1850s, settlers moving west followed the—

ⓕ Erie Canal.

Ⓖ Oregon Trail.

ⓗ Royal Road.

ⓙ Northwest Passage.

5 *Tom Thumb* proved that—

ⓐ steam-powered railroad engines were faster than horses.

ⓑ locomotives were undependable.

Ⓒ steam-powered railroad cars had better pulling power than horses.

ⓓ trains needed much improvement to be practical.

Regional Disagreements

Directions Read the passage below. Then fill in the chart that follows, showing the differences between the North and South.

The North and the South could not come to an agreement about slavery. Northerners did not think that slavery should be allowed to spread to the western territories, while Southerners thought they had the right to take their enslaved workers west with them—just as they would take their other property.

The Northern economy relied on manufacturing and shipping, not agriculture, so the North did not need laborers as the South did. Also, many Northerners thought that slavery was wrong and should be abolished, or done away with. Those Northerners were called abolitionists, and they wanted all people to be free. Even Northerners who were not abolitionists did not want more slave states added to the country.

However, the economy of the South depended on laborers. Plantation owners were able to harvest more cotton, indigo, and tobacco by using slaves to work in the fields. Those Southerners believed that individual states had the right to decide whether people could have slaves.

	North	**South**
Economy based on	manufacturing and shipping	farming
Viewed slavery as	wrong	a necessity to work the fields
Ideas about extending slavery	No more slave states should come into the nation.	States had the right to decide whether people could own slaves.

Directions Use the passage and chart above to answer the questions.

1 What were Northerners called who did not agree with slavery? Why were they called that? abolitionists; the word *abolition* means "the act of doing away with," so abolitionists wanted to do away with slavery.

2 Where did most Northerners believe slavery should not be allowed to spread? the western territories

Name _____ Date _____

Directions **Read the material below and then answer the questions.**

Henry Clay

When Missouri asked to be a state in 1819, Henry Clay was a congress member from Kentucky. Although Clay owned slaves, he did not want slavery to divide the country. He worked very hard to find a solution that would make both the North and the South happy. While other members of Congress were arguing for their region of the country, Clay said, "I know no South, no North, no East, no West, to which I owe any allegiance [loyalty]." His solution was called the Missouri Compromise.

John Quincy Adams

John Quincy Adams, a Northerner, was the secretary of state at the time. Adams kept a diary, and in February 1820 he wrote about what he thought the future might bring, "... if the dissolution [breaking apart] of the Union should result from the slave question, it is as obvious as anything... that it must shortly afterwards be followed by the universal emancipation [freeing] of the slaves..."

1 What viewpoint did Henry Clay have about the Union? How do you know?

Clay thought that the Union was more important than any one region of the

country. He said he was not loyal to any one section of the country.

_____

2 What did John Quincy Adams think would happen if the Union broke apart?

Shortly afterwards, all slaves would be freed.

Name _____ Date _____

Slavery and Freedom

Directions On the blanks provided, write the word or name that best completes each sentence. Some letters in your answers will have numbers under them. Write these letters in the appropriate boxes below, and you will find the name of the most famous conductor of the Underground Railroad.

1 A man named <u>N a t</u> <u>T u r n e r</u> led the first slave rebellion.
                   7

2 Something done in secret is done <u>u n d e r g r o u n d</u>.
                         3

3 A person who is running away is a <u>f u g i t i v e</u>.
                   9

4 To act against slavery is to <u>r e s i s t</u> it.
              4

5 The Virginia legislature debated the <u>e m a n c i p a t i o n</u>, or freeing, of slaves.
                  11   2

6 Sets of laws, known as slave <u>c o d e s</u>, ruled the lives of slaves.
                  6

7 Harriet Beecher Stowe wrote a book titled <u>U n c l e</u> <u>T o m's</u> <u>C a b i n</u>.
                         8   13

8 The newspaper *Freedom's Journal* called for <u>e q u a l i t y</u>, or equal rights for all people.
              12

9 Someone who wanted to end slavery was called an <u>a b o l i t i o n i s t</u>.
                  10   5

10 A former slave named <u>S o j o u r n e r</u> <u>T r u t h</u> traveled the country to speak out against slavery.
                      1

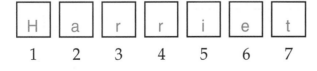
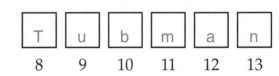

H	a	r	r	i	e	t		T	u	b	m	a	n
1	2	3	4	5	6	7		8	9	10	11	12	13

      Use after reading Chapter 12, Lesson 2, pages 444–449.

The Union Breaks Apart

Directions Read the passage below. Then read each statement that follows. If the statement is true, write *T* in the blank. If the statement is false, write *F* in the blank.

Abraham Lincoln had barely a year of formal schooling, but he learned to read and write. He was very intelligent and read everything he could. Growing up, Lincoln had many jobs such as a rail-splitter, riverboat man, store clerk, and postmaster. After studying very hard on his own, he finally became a lawyer.

About five years later, in 1842, Abe Lincoln married Mary Todd. Soon after, they purchased a home in Springfield, Illinois. The Lincolns had four sons, but only one lived past the age of 19.

In 1846, Lincoln was elected to the United States Congress, where he served one term in the House of Representatives. Fourteen years later, he was elected President of the United States. Lincoln is the only President to own a patent for an invention. In 1849 he patented a device for lifting boats up over shallow places in rivers. Lincoln was also presented with several honorary degrees during the time of the Civil War.

As respected and honored as President Lincoln was, Mrs. Lincoln was not very popular in Washington. She came from a Southern family, and four of her brothers were in the Confederate army. Some people feared Mary Lincoln was a Confederate spy.

___T___ **1** The Lincolns had four children.

___F___ **2** Mrs. Lincoln was well liked in Washington.

___T___ **3** Mrs. Lincoln had brothers in the Confederate army.

___F___ **4** Lincoln never owned a home of his own.

___T___ **5** Lincoln received several honorary degrees.

___F___ **6** Many presidents had inventions that they patented.

___F___ **7** Lincoln went to school for many years.

___F___ **8** Lincoln was elected to the United States Senate.

MAP AND GLOBE SKILLS

Compare Maps with Different Scales

Directions Look at the maps below, and then answer the questions on the facing page.

Map A: The Missouri Compromise, 1820

UNORGANIZED TERRITORY
MICHIGAN TERRITORY
MAINE
VT
NH
MA
CT
RI
NEW YORK
PENNSYLVANIA
NJ
INDIANA
OHIO
MD
DE
ILLINOIS
VIRGINIA
MISSOURI COMPROMISE LINE
MISSOURI
KENTUCKY
NORTH CAROLINA
TENNESSEE
SOUTH CAROLINA
ARKANSAS TERRITORY
ATLANTIC OCEAN
ALABAMA
GEORGIA
MISSISSIPPI
LOUISIANA
FLORIDA TERRITORY
Gulf of Mexico

Free state
Free territory
Admitted as a free state
Slave state
Slave territory
Admitted as a slave state
Missouri Compromise line
Present-day border

0   100   200 Miles
0   100 200 Kilometers

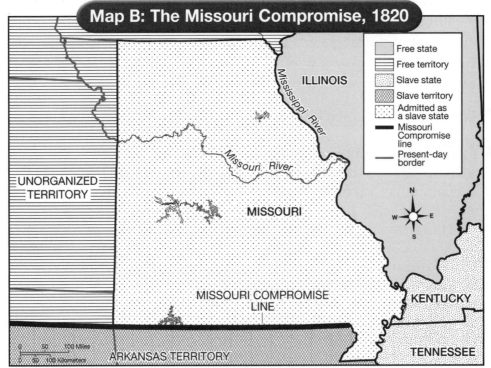

Map B: The Missouri Compromise, 1820

ILLINOIS
Mississippi River
Missouri River
UNORGANIZED TERRITORY
MISSOURI
MISSOURI COMPROMISE LINE
KENTUCKY
ARKANSAS TERRITORY
TENNESSEE

Free state
Free territory
Slave state
Slave territory
Admitted as a slave state
Missouri Compromise line
Present-day border

0   50   100 Miles
0   50 100 Kilometers

(continued)

Use after reading Chapter 12, Skill Lesson, pages 456–457.

Name _____ Date _____

Directions Use the maps on page 116 to answer the questions below.

1 Which map would be used to compare the size of Missouri to the size of Maine?

Map A _____

2 Which map would be used to determine the length of the border between

Missouri and Kentucky? Map B _____

3 How many slave states were there at the time of the Missouri Compromise?

11 _____

4 Was there more free territory or slave territory reserved?

free territory _____

5 Which state entered the Union at the same time as Missouri?

Maine _____

6 How many free states were there at the time of the Missouri Compromise?

11 _____

Directions Compare the two maps. Write *A* in the answer blank if Map A is more useful, and *B* if Map B is more useful.

___B___ **7** Determine the length of the part of the Mississippi River that forms a Missouri border.

___A___ **8** Determine whether the free or slave states had the largest land area.

___B___ **9** Determine the length of the part of the Missouri River that flows from the eastern border to the western border of Missouri.

___A___ **10** Determine the number of miles of border separating the free states and the slave states.

Civil War

Directions In the box provided, write a brief paragraph to explain why each item on the left was important to the Civil War.

Student responses will vary.
Possible responses are given.

EVENT	IMPORTANT BECAUSE

The Battle of Bull Run

The Battle of Bull Run was the first major battle fought between the Union and Confederacy. The Confederates won the battle, proving to the Northerners that the South was more powerful than they thought.

Anaconda Plan

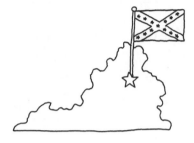

The purpose of the Union plan was to win control of the Mississippi River and blockade Confederate ports so that the South could not ship its cotton or bring in cash crops, it would not have money to buy supplies for its army.

The Battle of Antietam

Although the fighting at Antietam ended in nearly a tie, as a result of the battle President Lincoln announced his decision to issue an order freeing the slaves in areas that were still fighting against the Union.

The Emancipation Proclamation

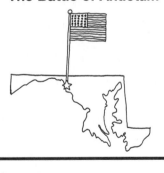

The presidential order said that all slaves living in those parts of the South still fighting against the Union would be freed. The Emancipation Proclamation also hurt the South's chances of getting help from Britain and France.

The Road to Union Victory

Directions Place the Civil War events in chronological order by numbering the dates on the time line.

1 Much of Atlanta burns to the ground after being captured by the Union army.

2 The Confederate army wins the Battle of Chancellorsville, and heads north towards Gettysburg.

3 The Union victory at the Battle of Gettysburg cripples the Confederate army.

4 General Robert E. Lee surrenders at Appomattox Court House, Virginia.

5 Lincoln gives the Gettysburg Address to inspire the nation and Union soldiers.

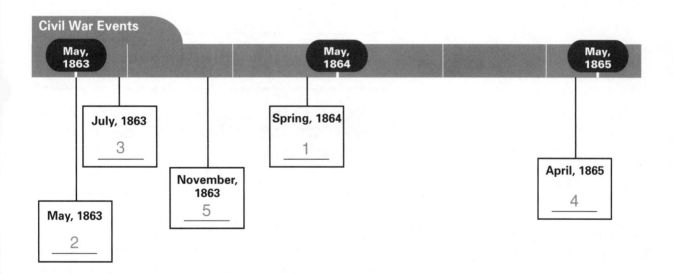

Civil War Events

| May, 1863 | | May, 1864 | | May, 1865 |

July, 1863 — 3

Spring, 1864 — 1

April, 1865 — 4

May, 1863 — 2

November, 1863 — 5

Important Leaders and Battles of the Civil War

Directions Complete this graphic organizer by categorizing important leaders and battles of the Civil War.

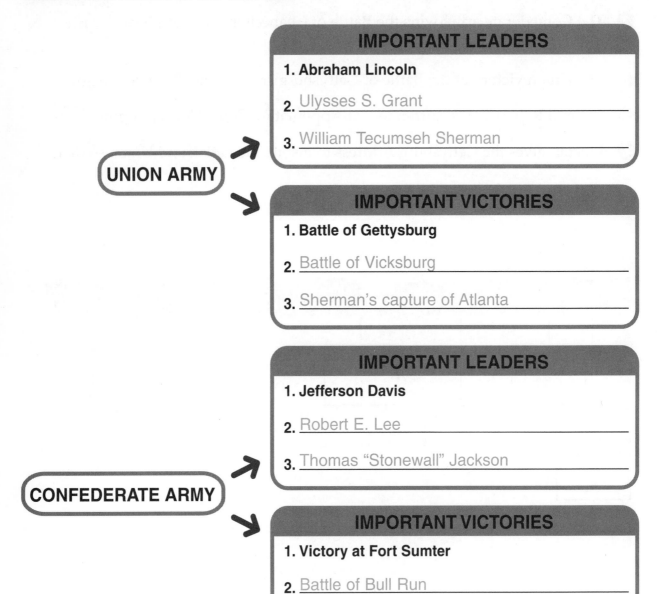

UNION ARMY

IMPORTANT LEADERS

1. **Abraham Lincoln**

2. Ulysses S. Grant

3. William Tecumseh Sherman

IMPORTANT VICTORIES

1. **Battle of Gettysburg**

2. Battle of Vicksburg

3. Sherman's capture of Atlanta

CONFEDERATE ARMY

IMPORTANT LEADERS

1. **Jefferson Davis**

2. Robert E. Lee

3. Thomas "Stonewall" Jackson

IMPORTANT VICTORIES

1. **Victory at Fort Sumter**

2. Battle of Bull Run

3. Battle of Chancellorsville

12 Test Preparation

Directions Read each question and choose the best answer. Then fill in the circle for the answer you have chosen. Be sure to fill in the circle completely.

1 Who was one of the men who persuaded Congress to accept the Missouri Compromise?
Ⓐ John Calhoun
Ⓑ Daniel Webster
Ⓒ Henry Clay
Ⓓ Abraham Lincoln

2 Who defended the rights of both slaves and women?
Ⓕ Elizabeth Cady Stanton
Ⓖ Harriet Beecher Stowe
Ⓗ Clara Barton
Ⓙ Mary Todd Lincoln

3 Abraham Lincoln became well known through his debates with—
Ⓐ Henry Clay.
Ⓑ Stephen Douglas.
Ⓒ Jefferson Davis.
Ⓓ Major Robert Anderson.

4 The Union strategy to win the war by weakening the South was called the—
Ⓕ Join or Die Plan.
Ⓖ slash and burn policy.
Ⓗ King Cotton policy.
Ⓙ Anaconda Plan.

5 How did Abraham Lincoln honor the dead at Gettysburg?
Ⓐ He set up a memorial fund.
Ⓑ He had a monument built at the cemetery.
Ⓒ He gave a speech at the cemetery.
Ⓓ He sent the Vice President to the battlefield.

Reconstruction

Directions Read the time line below of events surrounding Reconstruction. Then answer the questions that follow.

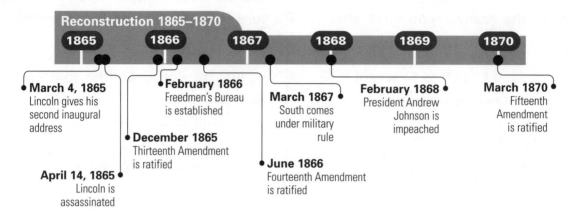

1 Was the Thirteenth Amendment ratified before or after President Lincoln gave his second inaugural address? _after_

2 What happened to President Abraham Lincoln on April 14, 1865?

He was assassinated.

3 About how many years passed between President Lincoln's assassination and President Johnson's impeachment? _three_

4 What two events shown on the time line both happened in the month of February? _The Freedmen's Bureau was established and President Johnson was impeached._

5 Was the Freedmen's Bureau established before or after the South came under military rule? _before_

6 How many constitutional amendments were passed between 1865 and 1870?

three

Name _____ Date _____

The South After the War

Directions Match each vocabulary word with its definition. Then use the vocabulary words to fill in the blanks of the sentences below.

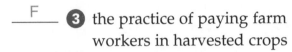

___D___ **1** former slaves

___B___ **2** government agency

___F___ **3** the practice of paying farm workers in harvested crops

___E___ **4** Northerners who went South during Reconstruction

___C___ **5** a method of voting in which no one knows for whom you voted

___A___ **6** separation of people based on race

A. segregation

B. bureau

C. secret ballot

D. freedmen

E. carpetbaggers

F. sharecropping

7 The _____secret ballot_____ is one of the most important parts of a fair election.

8 There are still many _____bureaus_____ in the United States government.

9 Life was hard for the _____freedmen_____ after the Civil War since few of them had enough money to buy their own land.

10 _____carpetbaggers_____ were given their name because of the suitcases many of them used to carry their belongings.

11 The practice of _____segregation_____ kept people apart in most public places.

12 Under the _____sharecropping_____ system most farmworkers found it difficult to make a living.

Settling the Last Frontier

Directions Study the map below.

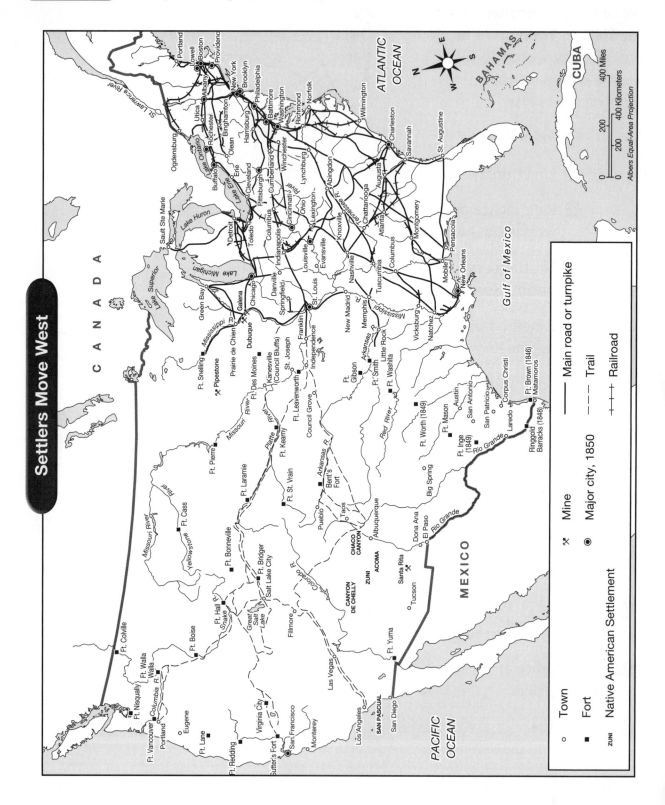

(continued)

Use after reading Chapter 13, Lesson 3, pages 486–491.

Name _____ Date _____

Directions Use the map and key on the preceding page to help you answer the questions. Write your answers in the blanks provided.

1 In what part of the country were most railroads located?

East _____

2 What Texas fort was the farthest west? Ft. Inge _____

3 In what parts of the country were most forts located? in the West and Midwest

_____

4 Could you travel by railroad from St. Louis, Missouri, to Salt Lake City?

no _____

5 How might you travel from Norfolk, Virginia, to Wilmington, North Carolina?

railroad or main road _____

6 Find the area that represents your state on the map. How settled was it? What might life have been like for the settlers who lived there?

Answers will vary. _____

_____

_____

_____

_____

Name _____ Date _____

CHART AND GRAPH SKILLS
Use a Climograph

Directions Look at the climograph of Austin, Texas, below. Then answer the questions on the blanks provided.

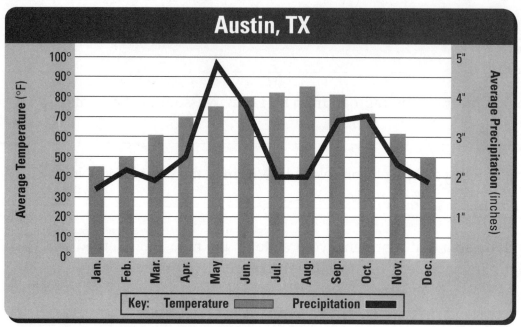

Source: National Drought Mitigation Center

(continued)

Use after reading Chapter 13, Skill Lesson, pages 492–493.

Name _____ Date _____

1 What is the average temperature in Austin in July? <u>about 82 degrees F</u>

2 What is the average precipitation in October? <u>about 3.5 inches</u>

3 Which three months are the driest? <u>January, March, December</u>

4 Which month is the coolest month? <u>January</u>

5 Which month is the warmest month? <u>August</u>

6 Which month gets the most precipitation? <u>May</u>

7 What do you observe about the months of July and August?

<u>They are nearly the same in both average temperature and rainfall.</u>

8 If you were driving cattle, what months do you think would be hardest on

people and cattle? What hardships might you face during the drive?

<u>Answers will vary but may include the wettest months, driest months, hottest</u>

<u>months, and coldest months. Hardships may include unexpected rainstorms,</u>

<u>drought, and extreme heat or cold.</u>

The Rise of New Industries

Directions Read the passages below, and answer the questions that follow.

In the 1800s the United States government made land grants to several railroad companies. More than 130 million acres were given to the Union Pacific, the Santa Fe, the Central and Southern Pacific, and the Northern Pacific railroads. In addition, western states gave the railroads 49 million acres. These land grants allowed the railroad industry to open new markets in the West for goods produced in the East.

One effect of the railroad boom was the need for stronger track. When the railroads were first built, the rails were made of iron. With the arrival of bigger and faster locomotives, however, these iron rails were not strong enough to withstand the weight of the new trains. A man named Henry Bessemer invented a way to make steel tracks strong enough for the larger locomotives. As a result, many companies were able to ship their products throughout the United States at a faster pace.

One company that used the new, faster trains to its advantage was Standard Oil. Founded by John D. Rockefeller in 1867, Standard Oil used the trains to ship oil all over the country. By 1882 Standard Oil controlled almost all of the oil refining and distribution in the United States.

1 Where did the railroad companies get the land on which they built the lines? The United States government and western states made land grants.

2 What effect did replacing iron rails with steel rails have on how United States companies could ship their products? Many United States companies could now ship their products at a faster pace.

3 What company did John D. Rockefeller found in 1867? Standard Oil

4 What role do you think the railroads played in the growth of Standard Oil? Standard Oil used the railroads to ship oil all over the United States. As a result, by 1882, the company controlled most of the oil distribution in the United States.

A Changing People

Directions Read the passage below and answer the questions that follow.

Irving Berlin's father was a cantor, a person who sings at religious services in Jewish synagogues. Perhaps it was his father's music that caused Berlin to be interested in writing songs. When he was in the Army during World War I, Berlin wrote a musical show. He later won both the United States Army's Award of Merit and a congressional medal for his songs. One of his most popular songs is "God Bless America."

Although Sophia Alice Callahan lived to be only 26 years old, she wrote an important novel. *Wynema: A Child of the Forest* is thought to be the first novel written by a Native American woman. Callahan's father was one-eighth Creek Indian. The novel has two major characters, Wynema and a Methodist teacher named Genevieve, who try to overcome prejudice against both Indians and women in the late nineteenth century.

Hiram Fong graduated from Harvard Law School before he returned to his native Hawaii to practice law. Hawaii at that time was still a territory. Fong served in the territorial legislature from 1938 to 1954. When Hawaii became a state, he was elected to the United States Senate. He served in the Senate from 1959 until 1977.

African American artist Jacob Lawrence did a 63-painting series on the lives of Harriet Tubman and Frederick Douglass. He studied painting in the Harlem section of New York City. During the depression, Lawrence worked for a federal project. This gave him enough money to be able to paint *Migration*, a series of 60 panels showing the movement of African Americans from the South to the North.

1 Explain what all the people in the passage have in common.

All were members of minority groups. Berlin was Jewish, Callahan was a

Native American woman, Fong was Asian, and Lawrence was African American.

2 Who might have influenced Irving Berlin's interest in music?

his father, who was a cantor

3 How did Hiram Fong serve his homeland? He was part of the territorial legislature

and a member of the Senate after Hawaii became a state.

4 What two series of paintings were created by Jacob Lawrence?

a series on Harriet Tubman and Frederick Douglass and a series titled *Migration,*

showing the movement of African Americans from the South to the North

Abraham Lincoln and Reconstruction

Directions Complete this graphic organizer by describing different points of view about Reconstruction.

WHO SAID IT	WHAT WAS SAID	WHY IT WAS SAID	POINT OF VIEW
Abraham Lincoln	"With malice toward none, with charity for all, with firmness in the right as God gives us to see the right, let us strive on to finish the work we are in, to bind up the nation's wounds…"	Because the country had been torn apart by the Civil War	Lincoln believed the South should not be punished for the Civil War and that the country should be brought back together peacefully and quickly.

WHO SAID IT	WHAT WAS SAID	WHY IT WAS SAID	POINT OF VIEW
Mary Chesnut	"Lincoln—old Abe Lincoln—killed… I know this foul murder will bring down miseries on us."	In response to Abraham Lincoln's assassination	Chesnut feared that, with the President gone, the South would now be held responsible for the Civil War and Lincoln's murder.

Use after reading Chapter 13, pages 475–507.

13 Test Preparation

Directions Read each question and choose the best answer. Then fill in the circle for the answer you have chosen. Be sure to fill in the circle completely.

1 Which of the following was **not** a condition for a Southern state's readmission to the Union?
  Ⓐ rewriting the state's constitution
  Ⓑ giving slaves some of the land
  Ⓒ ratifying the Thirteenth Amendment
  Ⓓ ratifying the Fifteenth Amendment

2 The most important work of the Freedmen's Bureau was—
  Ⓕ education.
  Ⓖ running the courts.
  Ⓗ helping people farm.
  Ⓙ rebuilding homes.

3 Which of the following was **not** a problem for homesteaders?
  Ⓐ drought
  Ⓑ range wars
  Ⓒ bitter cold and snow
  Ⓓ land costs

4 The last spike of the transcontinental railroad was driven at—
  Ⓕ Spokane, Washington.
  Ⓖ Promontory, Utah.
  Ⓗ Erie, Pennsylvania.
  Ⓙ St. Louis, Missouri.

5 The term "new immigration" refers to—
  Ⓐ people coming from Britain, Germany, and Ireland.
  Ⓑ African Americans moving north.
  Ⓒ people coming from Italy, Russia, and Greece.
  Ⓓ people coming from South America.

New Ideas and New Inventions

Directions Use the web diagram to answer the questions on page 133.

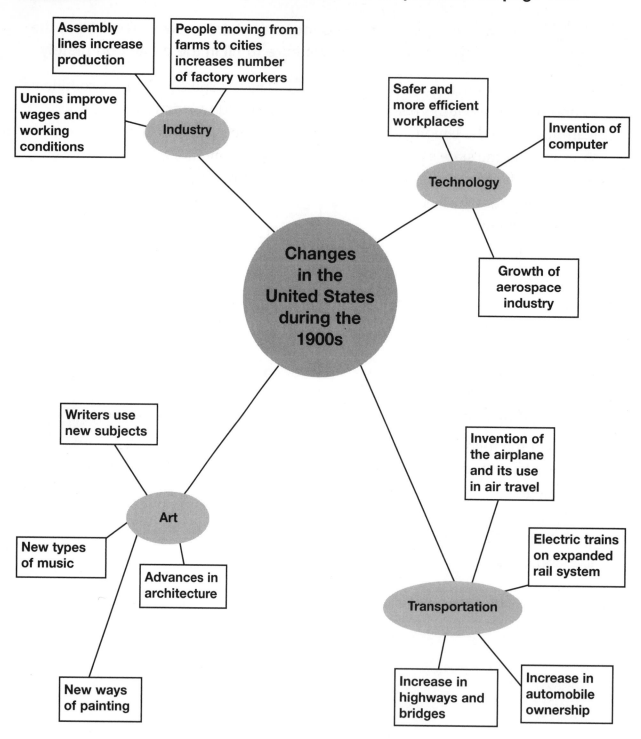

(continued)

Use after reading Chapter 14, Lesson 1, pages 524–531.

Name _____ Date _____

Directions Use the web diagram on page 132 to answer the questions below.

1 List the four major areas in which changes occurred during the 1900s.

art, industry, technology, transportation
_____

2 Which change in transportation resulted partly from the increase in the number of automobiles?

the increase in highways and bridges
_____

3 In which major area did advances make workplaces both safer and more efficient? technology

4 Which major advance in technology made space travel possible in the 1950s and 1960s?

Accept the invention of the computer or the

growth of the aerospace industry.

5 Use the diagram to describe how factories changed during the 1900s.

The number of factory workers increased as

people moved from farms to cities. The use of assembly lines increased

production. Workers organized labor unions to improve wages and working

conditions. Workplaces were made safer and more efficient.

6 List four areas of the arts in which changes took place during the 1900s.

music, painting, writing, architecture

Name _____ Date _____

MAP AND GLOBE SKILLS
Use a Time Zone Map

Directions Use the time zone map to answer the questions below.

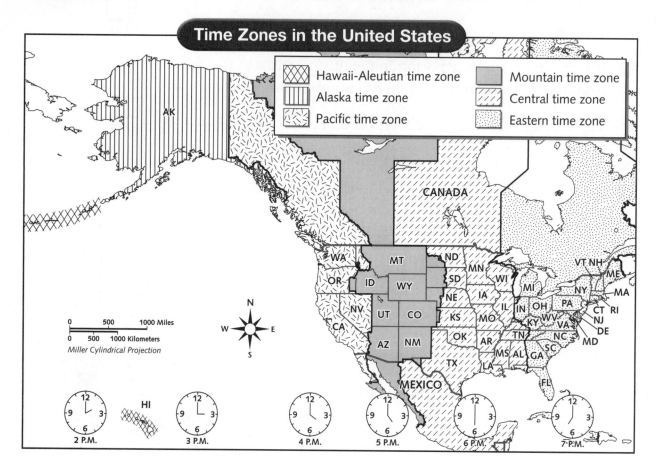

Time Zones in the United States

Hawaii-Aleutian time zone   Mountain time zone
Alaska time zone   Central time zone
Pacific time zone   Eastern time zone

2 P.M.   HI   3 P.M.   4 P.M.   5 P.M.   6 P.M.   7 P.M.

---

1 List the time zones of the United States, from east to west.

Eastern, Central, Mountain, Pacific, Alaska, Hawaii-Aleutian

2 If it is 1:00 P.M. in Virginia, what time is it in Florida? Explain your answer.

Florida is part of two time zones, so the answer depends on where you are. It is

1:00 P.M. in most of Florida. It is 12:00 P.M. in the far western part of the state.

3 How many time zones would you travel in if you flew from Georgia to California?

four

4 If you took a train from South Carolina to Illinois, would you have to set your

watch back (earlier) or ahead (later)? back or earlier

People on the Move

Directions Read the statements about immigration below. Then number the events from 1 to 8, starting with the event that happened first (1) and ending with the one that happened last (8). The numbers provided in annos are the correct answers students should give; the information following is for the teacher's use only.

___4___ About 50,000 Japanese immigrants came to states such as California and Hawaii in the first decade of the twentieth century. starting around 1900

___3___ The Chinese Exclusion Act said that Chinese workers could not enter the United States for ten years. act passed in 1882

___7___ Europeans came to the United States during World War II to escape the fighting. during the 1940s

___1___ Chinese immigrants started arriving in California before the Civil War and helped build western railroads. before 1860

___6___ There was a great decrease in the number of immigrants coming into the United States. after Immigration Act of 1924

___8___ Mexican Americans became one of the fastest-growing immigrant groups in the United States. according to the 2000 census

___5___ The Immigration Act limited the number of people allowed to move to the United States. act passed in 1924

___2___ Immigration patterns shifted from people mostly from western and northern Europe to people mostly from eastern and southern Europe. starting in the 1880s

Use after reading Chapter 14, Lesson 2, pages 534–541.

MAP AND GLOBE SKILLS
Use a Cartogram

Directions Use the political map and the population cartogram to answer the questions on page 137.

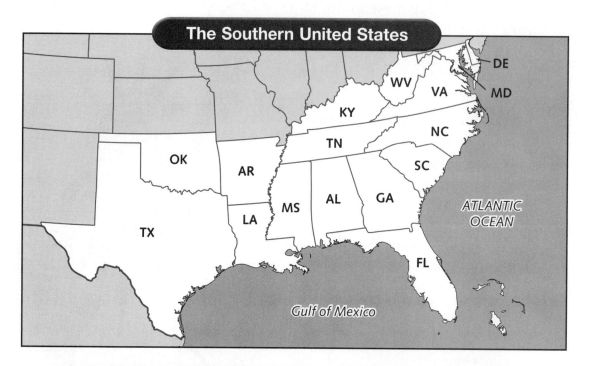

The Southern United States

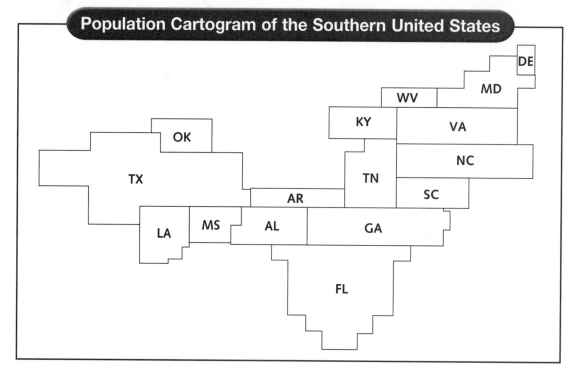

Population Cartogram of the Southern United States

(continued)

Use after reading Chapter 14, Skill Lesson, pages 542–543.

Name _____ Date _____

Directions Use the political map and the population cartogram on page 136 to answer the questions below.

1 Both the map and the cartogram compare the "size" of several states. Explain how size on the map is different from size on the cartogram.

"Size" on the political map refers to the land areas of the states. "Size" on the cartogram refers to the population of each state.

2 Which state is the smallest in land area: Alabama, Georgia, South Carolina, or Virginia? South Carolina

3 Which two states have the largest populations? Florida and Texas

4 What does the cartogram tell you about West Virginia and Delaware that you could not tell by their sizes on the political map? West Virginia is much larger than Delaware on the political map, but it is only a little larger on the cartogram. This shows that, although West Virginia is much larger in area, it has a population that is only slightly larger than Delaware's.

5 Alabama, Georgia, and Mississippi are all about the same size on the political map. Are their populations also about the same? Explain. The cartogram shows that Georgia has the largest population of the three. The populations of Alabama and Mississippi are closer to one another, but Alabama's population is larger.

6 Identify another characteristic of the states that you could compare with a cartogram. Accept all reasonable answers, which could include average or median income, average or median age, number of children in school, number of people in a certain ethnic or religious group, number of acres of farmland, and so on.

Name ______________________ Date ____________

Society Changes

Directions **Use the names in the box to correctly fill in the chart below.**

Susan B. Anthony	Dr. Martin Luther King, Jr.
Cesar Chavez	Robert M. La Follette
W.E.B. Du Bois	Janet Reno
Samuel Gompers	Theodore Roosevelt

labor leader who headed the American Federation of Labor and led strikes that won better pay and working conditions for American workers	1 Samuel Gompers
helped found the NAACP, an organization that works for equal rights for African Americans	2 W.E.B. Du Bois
leader of the movement for women's suffrage in the United States	3 Susan B. Anthony
founder of the National Farm Workers Association, which works for the rights of migrant farm workers	4 Cesar Chavez
African American civil rights leader who gave a memorable speech at a 1963 gathering in Washington, D.C.	5 Dr. Martin Luther King, Jr.
worked to bring the first primary elections to Wisconsin voters, giving people more power to choose their leaders	6 Robert M. La Follette
gave the American people the Square Deal in which the United States government helped citizens	7 Theodore Roosevelt
the first woman to be appointed attorney general of the United States	8 Janet Reno

Use after reading Chapter 14, Lesson 3, pages 544–551.

A United Country

Directions Match each constitutional amendment with its description. Write the correct letter of the description in the space provided.

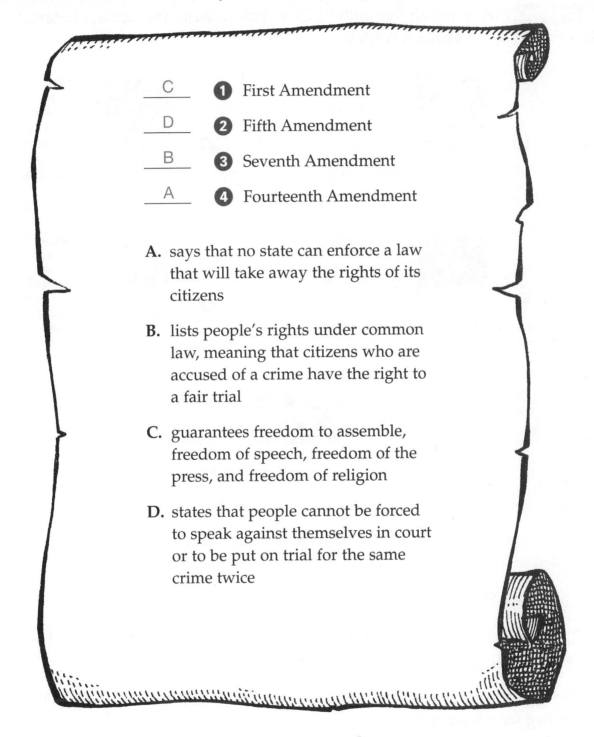

   C   **1** First Amendment

   D   **2** Fifth Amendment

   B   **3** Seventh Amendment

   A   **4** Fourteenth Amendment

A. says that no state can enforce a law that will take away the rights of its citizens

B. lists people's rights under common law, meaning that citizens who are accused of a crime have the right to a fair trial

C. guarantees freedom to assemble, freedom of speech, freedom of the press, and freedom of religion

D. states that people cannot be forced to speak against themselves in court or to be put on trial for the same crime twice

Name _____ Date _____

Identify Political Symbols

Directions Match each flag with its description. Write the correct letter of the description in the space provided.

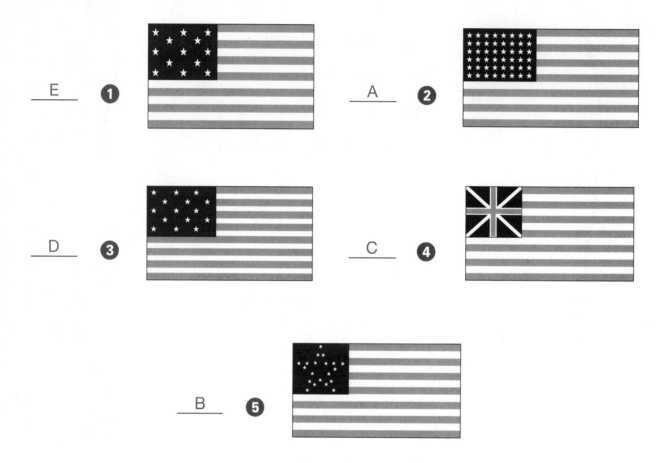

E **1**	A **2**
D **3**	C **4**
B **5**	

A. This flag flew over the United States between 1912 and 1959. Two stars were added to it in 1959, when Alaska and Hawaii became states.

B. The "Great Star Flag" of 1818 had a star for each of the 20 states.

C. The "Continental Colors" flew during much of the American Revolution. One symbol on the flag showed a connection to Great Britain.

D. The flag of 1795 had a star and a stripe for every state. It had more stripes than the flag we use today.

E. This flag, used when the United States first became an independent nation, had one stripe and one star for each of the original states.

Name _____ Date _____

Changes in Transportation and Population

Directions Complete this graphic organizer by predicting outcomes about changes in transportation and population.

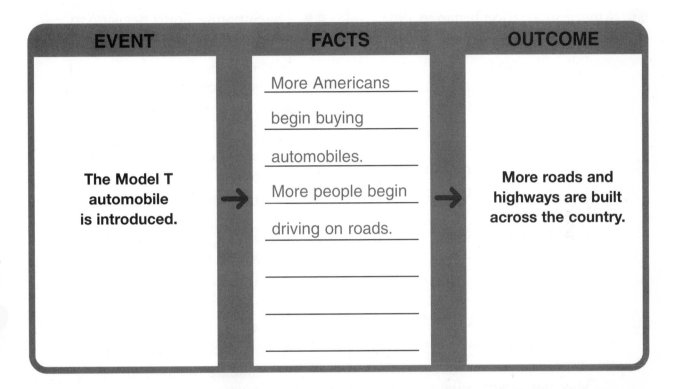

EVENT	FACTS	OUTCOME
The Model T automobile is introduced.	More Americans begin buying automobiles. More people begin driving on roads.	**More roads and highways are built across the country.**

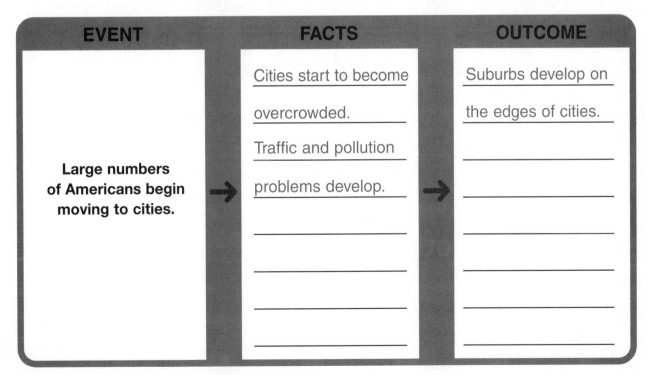

EVENT	FACTS	OUTCOME
Large numbers of Americans begin moving to cities.	Cities start to become overcrowded. Traffic and pollution problems develop.	Suburbs develop on the edges of cities.

Name _____ Date _____

14 Test Preparation

Directions Read each question and choose the best answer. Then fill in the circle for the answer you have chosen. Be sure to fill in the circle completely.

1 American aviation began in 1903 with the flight of—
Ⓐ John Glenn, Jr.
Ⓑ the Lindbergh brothers.
Ⓒ the Wright brothers.
Ⓓ Neil Armstrong.

2 After 1892, most immigrants came to the United States through—
Ⓕ Manhattan.
Ⓖ the Channel Islands.
Ⓗ Ellis Island.
Ⓙ Roosevelt Island.

3 Before Oklahoma became a state in 1907, its eastern section was set aside for—
Ⓐ Mexican immigrants.
Ⓑ Native Americans.
Ⓒ white settlers.
Ⓓ endangered Great Plains animals.

4 The Supreme Court decision in *Brown v. Board of Education of Topeka, Kansas*—
Ⓕ gave women the right to vote.
Ⓖ opened all-white public schools to African American children.
Ⓗ helped defeat anti-immigration laws.
Ⓙ made child labor illegal.

5 The phrase *e pluribus unum*, which appears on United States coins, emphasizes that—
Ⓐ the United States is a wealthy nation.
Ⓑ many individual Americans make up one nation.
Ⓒ the United States will always stand united.
Ⓓ all citizens have the right to free speech.

Use after reading Chapter 14, pages 522–559.

The United States Grows

Directions Name each numbered location on the map and describe an event in U.S. history related to it. Use the matching numbered lines provided. Possible responses below.

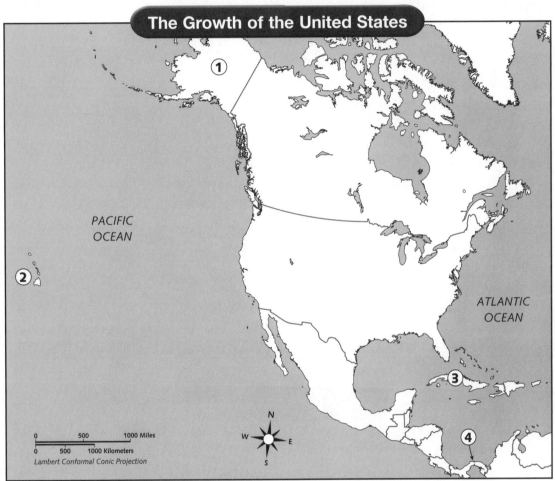

The Growth of the United States

PACIFIC OCEAN

ATLANTIC OCEAN

0   500   1000 Miles
0   500   1000 Kilometers
Lambert Conformal Conic Projection

N
W   E
S

1 Alaska; the United States buys Alaska in 1867; gold is found in the Klondike in 1896; Alaska becomes a territory in 1912; Alaska becomes the forty-ninth state in 1959.

2 Hawaii; the United States takes control of Hawaii in 1893; Hawaii becomes a United States territory in 1898; Hawaii becomes the fiftieth state in 1959.

3 Cuba; in 1898 the United States declares war on Spain; Americans fight in Cuba during the Spanish-American War.

4 Panama; the United States builds the Panama Canal between 1904 and 1914; the United States returns control of the canal to Panama.

MAP AND GLOBE SKILLS
Compare Map Projections

Map A: Europe, 1914

Azimuthal Equal-Area Projection

Map B: Europe, 1914

Mercator Conformal Projection

(continued)

Name _____ Date _____

Directions Study the conformal projection and equal-area projection maps on page 144. For each description below, put a check mark in the column for which the description is true. Some descriptions will be true for both projections. All descriptions will be true for at least one projection.

Conformal Projection	Equal-Area Projection	
✔	✔	**1** Shows the nations of Europe in 1914
	✔	**2** Shows the way Earth's surface curves
✔		**3** Uses straight lines for all lines of latitude and longitude
✔		**4** Shows all lines of latitude and longitude at right angles to each other
✔	✔	**5** Shows national borders
	✔	**6** Shows most of the Ottoman Empire
✔		**7** Uses a straight line for the prime meridian
✔		**8** Shows directions correctly
✔	✔	**9** Shows parallels *not* intersecting
	✔	**10** Shows correctly the sizes of nations compared with one another
✔		**11** Shows lines of latitude farther apart at the North Pole
	✔	**12** Uses curved lines to show latitude
✔		**13** Uses parallel lines to show longitude
	✔	**14** Shows lines of longitude closer together toward the North Pole
✔		**15** Shows all meridians the same distance apart
	✔	**16** Changes the shapes of nations

Defending Democracy

Directions Several causes and effects are listed in the box. Use them to fill in the graphic organizer below.

- In a compromise, the Soviet Union and the United States reach an agreement over missiles in Cuba.
- The United States enters World War I on the side of the Allied Powers.
- Japanese planes attack Pearl Harbor in 1941.
- Communism spreads in Europe and Asia after World War II.

CAUSE	➡	EFFECT

1 Japanese planes attack Pearl Harbor in 1941. ➡ **The United States enters World War II on the side of the nations fighting Germany, Italy, and Japan.**

2 Communism spreads in Europe and Asia after World War II. ➡ **The United States and its allies fight against communism.**

3 **German submarines sink several United States ships in 1917.** ➡ The United States enters World War I on the side of the Allied Powers.

4 **President Kennedy orders a naval blockade of Cuba to stop the Soviet Union from setting up missiles there.** ➡ In a compromise, the Soviet Union and the United States reach an agreement over missiles in Cuba.

(continued)

Use after reading Chapter 15, Lesson 2, pages 576–583.

Name _____ Date _____

Directions Write a sentence explaining
how each effect on the previous page helped
defend democracy.

The order of students' answers may vary.

5 The United States helped defeat the forces

of Nazi Germany and Japan, stopping those

nations from taking over many countries in

Europe, Africa, and Asia.

_____

_____

6 By fighting to keep the Soviet Union from

gaining control of other countries, the United

States and its allies limited the spread of

communism during the Cold War years after

World War II.

_____

7 The participation of the United States in World War II helped the Allies defeat

Germany and preserve democracy and liberty in Europe.

_____

_____

8 War between the United States and the Soviet Union was avoided, and a

Soviet military threat to the United States was removed from Cuba.

_____

_____

_____

A World Superpower

Directions Match the name of each leader listed in the box with the description of his action below.

George Bush	George W. Bush
Bill Clinton	John F. Kennedy
Colin Powell	Ronald Reagan
Franklin D. Roosevelt	

Colin Powell ___ **1** He planned the military strategy for the Persian Gulf War.

Franklin D. Roosevelt ___ **2** This President helped establish the United Nations.

Bill Clinton ___ **3** He proposed the North American Free Trade Agreement during his presidency.

George Bush ___ **4** While President, he organized a group of nations to fight Saddam Hussein after the Iraqi invasion of Kuwait.

Ronald Reagan ___ **5** As President, he focused on providing aid to private businesses in other countries.

John F. Kennedy ___ **6** The Peace Corps was started during his presidency.

George W. Bush ___ **7** He spoke before Congress following the terrorist attacks on the United States in 2001.

(continued)

Use after reading Chapter 15, Lesson 3, pages 586–593.

Name _____ Date _____

Directions **Using the lines provided, write a short description of how the
action of each leader on page 148 has affected the United States.**
The order of students' answers may vary.

8 Colin Powell; The United States earned a quick victory in the conflict, increasing

its power and prestige.

_____

9 Franklin D. Roosevelt; Membership in the United Nations allowed the United

States to work with other nations to maintain international peace and security.

_____

10 Bill Clinton; Companies in the United States formed partnerships with companies

in Canada and Mexico.

_____

11 George Bush; This action restored the balance of power in the Middle East and

kept oil resources that were important to the United States out of Iraq's control.

_____

12 Ronald Reagan; The plan served to help the economies of allies of the

United States.

_____

13 John F. Kennedy; The program allowed American citizens to learn about and

help people in need in other nations.

_____

14 George W. Bush; Citizens of the United States united to make sure that their

country remains free and strong.

_____

CITIZENSHIP SKILLS
Make Economic Choices

Directions Imagine that you have $25 to spend. You must choose between buying a savings bond, which will increase in value to $30 over a certain number of years, and buying another item you would like to own. Complete the graphic organizer below to help you make an economic choice.

CHOICES
Name a $25 item you would like to buy.

United States savings bond

Students may name any item that costs about $25.

OPPORTUNITY COSTS

If you buy the savings bond, you will not be able to buy the other item you want.

If you buy the other item, you will not make the $5 the savings bond will earn.

ECONOMIC CHOICE

Compare the value of what you will be giving up, or the opportunity cost, for each choice. When you have made your decision, your other choice becomes your trade-off. Write which item you will buy.

Students should list the savings bond or the other item.

Use after reading Chapter 15, Skill Lesson, pages 594–595.

Facts and Opinions About Alaska and Hawaii

Directions Complete this graphic organizer by identifying facts and opinions about Alaska and Hawaii.

ALASKA

FACT   **OPINION**

The purchase of Alaska increased the size of the United States by almost 20 percent.

Alaska is the best state in

which to live.

FACT   **OPINION**

On January 3, 1959, Alaska

became the 49th state.

The purchase of Alaska was

foolish.

HAWAII

FACT   **OPINION**

The first people to live in

Hawaii were travelers from

the South Pacific.

Hawaii has the best climate.

FACT   **OPINION**

On August 20, 1959, Hawaii became the 50th state.

The hula dance is easy to do.

Name _____ Date _____

15 Test Preparation

Directions Read each question and choose the best answer. Then fill in the circle for the answer you have chosen. Be sure to fill in the circle completely.

1 Which late-nineteenth-century war expanded United States territory?
- Ⓐ the Mexican-American War
- Ⓑ the Civil War
- Ⓒ the Spanish-American War
- Ⓓ World War I

2 The United States carried on a cold war against the Soviet Union to stop the spread of—
- Ⓕ the Axis Powers.
- Ⓖ global trade.
- Ⓗ communism.
- Ⓙ all of the above.

3 Which of the following countries did the United States defeat during World War II but not during World War I?
- Ⓐ France
- Ⓑ Japan
- Ⓒ Germany
- Ⓓ Russia

4 The purpose of NATO today is to—
- Ⓕ fight dictatorships in North Africa.
- Ⓖ create security and stability in Europe.
- Ⓗ feed the hungry in developing nations.
- Ⓙ provide weapons to all United States allies.

5 In the 1990s the United States helped restore peace to—
- Ⓐ Russia and Korea.
- Ⓑ Kuwait and Kosovo.
- Ⓒ Albania and Rwanda.
- Ⓓ Yugoslavia and South Africa.

Use after reading Chapter 15, pages 564–595.